The Inner Chamber
Cornerstones of Magickal Practice

Volume One
It's Written in the Stars
Astrology

Robin Fennelly

The Inner Chamber
Volume One
It's Written in the Stars

It's Written in the Stars is the first book in The Inner Chamber Series

All rights reserved. No part of this book may be reproduced or transmitted in any form or by any means, electronic or mechanical, including photocopying, recording or by any informational retrieval system without permission in writing from the author except for brief quotes used in reviews or scholarly work.

Copyright © 2012 by Robin Fennelly
ISBN 978-1-105-41875-4

Cover Art: Caitlin Fennelly, M.F.A.

Bound and Printed in the United States

Dedication

In dedication to my Mother, Jeanne who provided a loving home and open environment to explore the varied spiritual paths.

In dedication to my Husband, Ned who has supported my dreams and allowed me to pursue my chosen path.

In dedication to my five wonderful Children, Kyle, Jenny, Eryn, Caitlin and Jessica who taught me patience and nurturing and allowed me the privilege of helping them find their own destinies.

In dedication to the Elders and community of like minded Spirits that is The Assembly of the Sacred Wheel where I have learned, taught and grown.

In dedication to the Adepts and many fine Teachers of the diverse Spiritual Paths who are I am honored to call Friend and who live the Truth that all Paths lead to the One.

Table of Contents

Introduction	7
The Four Elements	9
The Three Modalities	18

Part One: The Signs of the Zodiac — 25

Aries	27
Taurus	30
Gemini	33
Cancer	36
Leo	39
Virgo	43
Libra	47
Scorpio	51
Sagittarius	55
Capricorn	59
Aquarius	62
Pisces	66

Part Two: Temple of Stars Pathworkings — 69

How to use the Pathworkings	71

The Hall of Aries	73
The Hall of Taurus	76
The Hall of Gemini	80
The Hall of Cancer	83
The Hall of Leo	87
The Hall of Virgo	89
The Hall of Libra	91
The Hall of Scorpio	94
The Hall of Sagittarius	97
The Hall of Capricorn	100
The Hall of Aquarius	102
The Hall of Pisces	104

INTRODUCTION

About The Series

It's Written in the Stars is the first volume in the series **The Inner Chamber.** These books are meant to serve as glimpses into the cornerstones of a well structured magickal practice. The topics that will be covered in each volume comprise the basic information that should be incorporated into a diverse and well-rounded study of magick and the related arts.

Each subject will be referenced through poetry, prose and pathworkings or suggested exercises in accord with the specific material. These books are not meant to serve as an in depth study, but rather to whet the appetite for more thorough exploration as you are called and feel resonance to.

About Volume One

This book is separated into Two Parts. Part One discusses the attributes of each of the Twelve Astrological signs of the Zodiac. Part Two offers Twelve Pathworkings, each relating to one of the Twelve Zodiacal signs. These can be used in future studies or stand alone as a meditative tool to open yourself to each of the twelve signs' energetic nature.

You will find that the study of astrology is first and foremost a study of yourself. Your strengths, your weaknesses and the potential that was written in your cosmic blueprint on the day and at the hour you were born. My studies began with my own natal chart. Step by step revealing and peeling back the layers of information and then making application and drawing new conclusions from the information I found within the natal charts of my family. What began as a cursory study to use for personal exploration developed into a method of overlay onto my magickal practice and workings. Using the astrological information and selecting the appropriate date, the most potent time of the day and the energy of specific astrological components added a layer of complexity which deepened the energetic support, and caused potent outcome.

It has been many years of study that has brought me to the point of feeling secure in the information I have gathered and ready to share it with others. My hope is that this little book will ignite the passion within you to look at yourself through the lens of the Cosmos. For once you have the briefest glimpse of what potential lay in waiting, you will never quite look at the world or the people within it in the same way.... RCF

Each of the astrological signs is identified by two basic qualities: the element (Earth, Air, Fire or Water) to which it resonates and the quality of that particular element (Cardinal, Fixed or Mutable).

The Four Elements

The Elements of Earth, Air, Fire and Water relate to the basic nature of the astrological sign and the manner in which the sign expresses itself. Earth signs tend towards a more physical, material and grounded approach. Air signs rely on their mental processes to navigate through varied situations. Fire signs tend to be action and goal oriented; consistently driven by strong passions and determined will. And, Water signs operate from the place of emotions and tend to follow a more intuitive path.

These Four basic elements are the fundamental ingredients contained within every structure of our Cosmos. Planets, stars, and all life forms are combinations of all the basic elements. They may have one or more of the elements in dominance, but there is always a thread of connection with those elements that are not as overt that enables the more dominant to exist. At a physical level the elements are all around us in the forms of the air we breathe, the water we drink, the food we eat and the energy that we exert to accomplish a task.**

**Note: There are 5 elements in esoteric and spiritual practice. Spirit-being the fifth- is not attributed to any of the astrological signs. I see Spirit as holding the place of Humanity, or those who we are creating the astrological blue print for. In this way, Spirit is contained in all attributions of a person's astrological make-up as our bodies hold each of the five elements within our very being.

The Fire Signs
Aries - Leo - Sagittarius

The South - Transformation – Will

Fire signs are those of action, determination and catalytic energy. Their nature is that of inspiration and igniting any situation with enthusiasm and creative solution. In the sign of Aries, fire takes the role of being catalyst, novice and eager participant. Aries is the first sign of the zodiac and as such provides the younger perspective of all acceptance and anticipation of what lay around every corner. The sun shines ever so brightly on the natives of the Fire signs and non-is more brilliantly lit than that of Leo, the Lion and heart of the Sun. Fire signs enjoy attention and being in the spotlight which makes them good candidates for roles of leadership or trail blazing. Similar to physical fire, if that enthusiasm and drive is not carefully tended and guided it will destroy everything in its path in a non-productive volatile nature. The fiery nature of Sagittarius is one of enthusiasm and spreading the fires of that enthusiasm far and wide. Just as the archer sends multiple arrows out in search of the precise point of the bull's eye, so too Sagittarians share the will to action with all they meet, setting the fires of action as lanterns along the path.

Esoterically: FIRE, unlike the other elements cannot exist in physical form without consuming and destroying something else, thus causing transformation of that thing. It is out of that destruction that the potential for the most growth often occurs. Like the legendary Phoenix rising from the flames of ash.

At a purely mundane and physical level Fire is associated with heat. The warmth of the Sun and the heat of the wood stove that keeps us warm in wintry weather. When we take it to the mental level, Fire becomes the passion that excites and ignites. It is the catalyst that creates movement and it is the creative spark that leads to new invention or manifest creation. At a spiritual level, Fire carries the seeds of transformation that are the stuff of initiatory change, action and development of the Higher Will.

Forged by Fire

Crackle and hiss
The verbosity of flame's intent
The cold gives way to passion
And desire's deep intent.

Step into the flame
Let the heat transform
The ash of Phoenix rises
Only after the charged
Embrace of will and desire.

The embers burn low
And I am called to tend their need
To keep the fires burning
To fan the flame within.
And throughout the dark night
The light from fire's core
Holds me deep within her grasp til
Father Sun rises
Jubilant at Dawn's waking.

The Earth Signs

Taurus - Virgo - Capricorn

The North – Strength- Foundation

The energy of the Earth signs is that of solid foundation and connection to the physical world. Money, material comforts and concerns and a very straight forward, no nonsense approach are typical of these signs. Expressed through Taurus, earth presents in a stalwart and at times stubborn approach, remaining steadfast and strong in conviction and opinion. In the sign of Virgo, this earthy nature presents in a calculating and organized perspective that enables the native of this sign to analyze, sort through and come to reasonable and well-thought conclusions. Planning and strategizing are strong suits of Virgo. Expressed through Capricorn, the ability to remain fully present and be thinking ahead with concrete plans and ideas is the natural tendency. Also being Cardinal Earth, the caution is that things are at times slow to form, but once conceptualized and then brought into fruition; they are also extremely difficult to dismantle. Similar to pushing the wagon uphill, but once the crest has been reached, the downhill momentum can be difficult to control.

Esoterically: Earth is associated with the cardinal direction of the North, the place of midnight, when the sun's light has moved beyond the horizon of sight and appears to be held in the darkness of night before sunrise. Earth is also associated with all things of the physical realm. Humanity, flora, fauna, crystal and more are all contained within earth. Earth is the place of manifestation, concrete and tangible outcome. Earth holds within its bound the potential for creation, evolution and sustaining of what has been created. Earth is the energy of the magnet that attracts to itself what it sends forth. Because earth defines the manifest world and all that is contained within, it draws to itself the power of manifestation itself.

Dig Deeply

Dig deeply
Soil soft and fertile seeds
Ready to sprout.

Stand strong on foundation
That rises up to meet
The curve of foot.

Support of unwavering
Might as all who Stretch
Towards the heavens
Stay anchored on
Her solid ground.

Mountain and stone
Physical body and Manifest
World just beneath my feet
And swirling all around.

Dig deeply
Center your focus
And know that
All your endeavors
Will flourish
When you send your roots
Down deeply.

Air
Gemini - Libra - Aquarius

The East – Mind – Intellect

The Air signs fully embrace and thrive in the mental realms. Interactions are first thought through looking for points of inspiration and logic. Expressed through Gemini, this air presents in rapid-fire debate, discussion, action and decision making. Communication of all form is the tool of the Gemini native, wielding it like the most skilled of swordsmen and cutting through any hesitation. In Libra, air and intellect flow from a sense of civility, equity and refinement. The balance of the scales of Libra is not one of equal weight, but rather that of the balance that is achieved when the appropriate amount of grounding is counterpoised with the lightness of higher pursuits. And, in the sign of Aquarius, air soars to new and inventive heights. Invention and the ability to arrive from A-Z in a milli-second are the skills of this sign. Natives of Aquarius see the broadest perspective in all matters and are most at home in the mental worlds.

Esoterically: Air is associated with the cardinal direction of the East, the place of the rising sun or dawn. Air is also associated with mind and intellect, the place that gives rise to the birth of ideas. When we connect with the element of air we are moving through the realms of the mind and just as the breeze carries seeds from location to location that eventually become tree or plant, the seeds of bright ideas and inspiration are carried within the air-like movement of the mind.

I Am All

I am the essence of pure thought
I am the light that illuminates
The darkest caverns of the mind

I am what has passed and what
Will be in the depths of the elements.

I am both light and darkness
Wisdom and human ignorance
I am all that is
I am all that is.

I am that which probes
For inspiration and guides
You to falter and begin again
I am all and I am nothing.

I am All and I am nothing
Human and Divine beyond
The grasp of human mind
Beyond the grasp of human knowing.

I ward and bless the mind
Thought both evil and good
For from both spring the truth.

I am lightning
I am thunderbolt
I am the realms that
No mortal mind can dream upon.

I flow and ebb and retreat
Only to return with
Push of full force
All this I AM to
Allow YOU to
See the Divinity
Within.

Water
Cancer - Scorpio – Pisces

The West – Intuition – Emotions

The Water signs express themselves through the filter and guidance of emotions. These are the most intuitive of the signs and can also be the most emotionally overwrought if care is not taken to set boundaries in place. In the sign of Cancer, water is most at home moving with the ebb and flow of the moon's pace. Homebodies and loyal to a fault, Cancer natives seek connection at the deepest of emotional levels. Cancer is the first outpourings from the womb of creation. In the sign of Scorpio, the emotions have access to both the higher and the lower realms of self. Scorpio natives have choice of either hiding as recluse and lashing out in defense or rising to the heights of the keen perception of the eagle or the ultimate expression as the Phoenix with the ability to navigate through any situation and use it as a lesson of transformation. In the watery sign of Pisces, this flow of emotions takes the stance of the loving elder or crone. Compassion and self-sacrifice are the natural way of being and boundaries often blur if another is in need. Pisces is the last sign of the zodiac, having reached the placed of traversing the energies of the other signs, having finally arrived at Pisces, wisdom is accumulated and the pearls of its product are offered to all.

Esoterically: Water is associated with the cardinal direction of the West, the place of the setting sun or dusk. It is both the place of endings and also the anticipation of the rising of the lunar energies as night falls. It is closely connected to the similar energies of the Moon and its impulse of ebb and flow, waxing and waning as it moves through its cycles of change. It is the emotional outpour and connection to the intent of mind and action of will that creates successful endeavors, all being held within the foundation of the element of earth. Water is also associated with the emotions and intuition. This is the place of wisdom of the information contained within that holds the spark of quickening (Fire) and nurtures and heals what calls to it's wisdom. Just as Fire is transformative through the energies of release and burning away that which is no longer needed, water transforms through healing and smoothing the roughened edges and following the depths of the intuitive, instinctual self.

Water at a physical level can cause erosion of the surfaces over which it passes. This erosion is a slow and cumulative process that often serves to change that surface by smoothing or wearing away to reveal what lies below. When we open to our emotional self, we allow the floodgates of inner truth to wash over, change, heal and transform what our mind of intellect has logically and rationally presented.

Mysterious Course

Follow the stream
As it weaves on its own
Mysterious course.

Moon rises and waters
Of life ebb and flow
Back to the shore of foundation.

Emotion wells up and
Spills out strongly changing
Everything in its path.

Relax into the current
And trust in the
Depth of its reach
The waters will heal
If you sink into their
Loving embrace.

The Three Modalities

> Cardinal = Becoming/Initiating
>
> Fixed = Stable/Solid
>
> Mutable = Flexible/Flowing

The Modalities of Cardinal, Fixed and Mutable chart a phase similar to that of the waxing, peak and waning of the moon. If you look carefully at the table (Fig. 1) you will see a pattern emerging. As the signs progress through the zodiac every 3 signs represent the trinity of the 3 modalities. This supports the flow of energy and natural progression from one sign to the next in reflecting its story of progression and evolution through the dynamics of the zodiac cycle. Additionally, each of the modalities has within its specific energy the four elements of Fire-Water-Air and Earth.

In their assignment to the astrological signs, the modalities become the foundational basic qualities of the sign that are enhanced and modified towards expression in a unique and specialized way. For example, the Air signs (Gemini, Libra and Aquarius) are all strongly guided and motivated by the mental processes, but the addition of the modalities gives a slightly different expression of that process to each of the three. In Cardinal (the initial outpour) Libra, the mental process is in its experimental stage of trial, test, change and seed of thought, thus the balance and weighing of each of the processes. In Fixed (stable and the foundation of middle way) Aquarius, that mental process can take more liberties, expand and move in all directions because it has gathered the necessary information from the initial seed thought to allow movement from a solid ground. And, finally in Mutable Gemini (flexibility, endings and beginnings), the mental process can either take root and expand from this place of center, die off in pursuit of a more refined or different route or be completely transformed.

Table of the Modalities (Fig. 1)

Sign	Quality	Element
Aries	Cardinal	Fire
Taurus	Fixed	Earth
Gemini	Mutable	Air
Cancer	Cardinal	Water
Leo	Fixed	Fire
Virgo	Mutable	Earth
Libra	Cardinal	Air
Scorpio	Fixed	Water
Sagittarius	Mutable	Fire
Capricorn	Cardinal	Earth
Aquarius	Fixed	Air
Pisces	Mutable	Water

The Cardinal Signs
Aries- Cancer- Libra and Capricorn

The Cardinal signs impart qualities which are those of initiating whatever they are exerting their energy upon. They are the stages of beginnings and initial outpour.

I bubble up
And push and strain
To make my
Presence known.

I am the first
Stirrings of a love
That will ignite into
A passionate journey.

I am the first spark
That takes root
Before it can spread
Into bonfire's blaze.

I am earth that shifts
And moves as new
Land and mountain's
Peak reaches up
Towards sky.

I am ember and droplet.
I am the first breath that
Gives life and the starting
Place of all manifest form.

I am the first drop
That multiplies and
Fills cavern's expanse
As strong river flows.

The Fixed Signs
Taurus- Leo- Scorpio and Aquarius

The Fixed signs are stable and the product of the initial burst of movement to a place of permanence and center point.

Hold steady
Stand strong
Be the container.

Hold fast the
Energy that pours
Forth relentlessly.

The Middle Way
Proves firm and true
What generates inside
Soars above and
Reaches deeply below.

Draw up its strength
Pull down its light
Draw in its anchor of center
And allow to pour forth that
Which will be renewed.

** It is worth noting that the Four Fixed Signs of the Zodiac are the astrological attributes of the Four Holy Creatures.

Taurus is the winged Bull- Earth
Scorpio is the Eagle - Water
Leo is the Winged Lion - Fire
Aquarius is the Winged Man- Air

The addition of wings to these creatures represents the elements of nature and man in their highest form and the aspirations and achievement of spiritual purpose having transcended the lower planes.

Wings beat
The Bull charges
Horns sharpened
Ready to claim its ground.

Wings beat
The Lion bellows in mighty roar
Claws sharpened as flames spark
As mighty paw strikes.

Wings beat
Eagle soars high above
Flame rises up to consume
And the Phoenix lifts
Pointed beak.

Arms reach upwards
Sacred breath spirals in
Heart beats the cosmic rhythm
And the Divine Human is born!

The Mutable Signs
Gemini- Virgo- Sagittarius and Pisces

The Mutable signs are those that are flexible in nature. Their movement is that of having come from a stable center point to a place of stretching towards endings, completion and anticipation of the next phase of new catalytic action.

Reaching out from
Refined stable space
Tentative strands
Gently probing spaces unknown.

You expand and contract
Labor pains birthing
A new way of Being.

The death of one
Will mean the birth of many
And so the cycle continues
Each ebbing and flowing
Into the next.

You have seen all
That has come forward
You have lapped at
The waters of pristine
Lake and sat in the
Locks that have
Pent up your energy.

And, now in the final
Stage of your expression
You heed the call of your
True nature.

Reach out from refined
Stable space and push
Against the self-imposed boundaries
Break free newly transformed
Cross the threshold and
Reenter the Dawn.

Part One

The Signs of the Zodiac

ARIES
♈

Cardinal - Fire

Planetary Ruler - Mars

Keywords

Pioneers

Dynamic Energy

Enthusiasm

Assertiveness

The Power of Exploration, Enthusiasm and Fresh Approach

The Path of Action

Birth Rite

Seed of New Beginnings
Time of sweet release
Breath of untainted newness
Tiny embers strewn beneath soft
Blanket of newborn's down.

Fingers dipping excitedly
Eagerly in all that can be found
Anticipation of new discoveries and
Child-like innocence fuels the
Thirst and inquisitive nature.

Of one who seeks a place
At the table of life's experience.

All turn towards the promise
Of life restored anew
And the quaternary of balance
Infused with Luna's light opens
The causeway after the challenge
Of being is sealed.

All hold pause and heed the warning
Of youth's impetuous step
The fool, signaling the issuance of
Travesty or achievement.

And, in the space of quiet calm
Between the contractions of labored new birth
The Universe holds vigil
As star and planet follow
Evolution's plan~ held in the rapture
Of consummate union.

Sparks of will come bursting forth and
Sphere of cobalt radiance crowns slowly
Mother Universe suckles youth at her breast
As Father Time waits patiently
The Celestial wheel moves once again within
The primordial womb.

Aries is the first sign of the Zodiac, and in holding this starting place can be equated with new life and the heralding of potential that has not yet acquired the experience of years and maturity in outlook. This is not to say that those under the influence of this sign are immature and lack experience, but rather that they bring a certain level of newness and innocence to any endeavor. The energy of Aries is that of looking out from the eyes of a curious child who sees multiple possibilities and new adventure everywhere bringing an inquisitive nature and youthful energy. Having the quality of a Cardinal Modality bolsters this enthusiastic nature for beginning new projects and looking at things through a fresh (and not yet biased) perspective.

Aries is a Fire sign. The energy of Fire is will to Action. In Aries this fire takes the form of the first sparks of flame that are not quite at their fullest, but hold the seed potential, and if directed and guided will go on to fuel the larger blaze. Being Cardinal Fire, there is a large boost of energy, will and action at the onset, but longevity, follow through and completion can sometimes be a problem as there is a natural interest in many paths and the exploration of too many interests can cause the initial flame to burn out.

Mars is the Ruling Planet of Aries. This is the combustible force that propels this sign forward. It is justifiable assertion of itself that puts the plan in motion and irrational aggressiveness that serves as the tantrum of a child wanting attention and not receiving what is needed, before they can move on to their next creative project.

TAURUS
♉

Fixed - Earth

Planetary Ruler - Venus

Keywords

Strength

Stability

Inertia

Manifestation

Physical

The Power of Determination, Assessment and Goals

The Path of Nature

A Fiercely Beating Heart

Strength unmoved as dust swirls
Around the stamping of hoof
Fire rages in the heart and
Coils of fevered breath move from
Chamber of lung and throat
Weaving between air's stagnant web.

I am earth, solid and great
In purpose and my strength
Is held and guided by a heart that beats
Fiercely to the rhythm of love.

I will stand my ground in
Defense of the truths I perceive.
And, if provoked will
Charge with intent and
Precise aim as I relentlessly
Pursue the source of irritation.

Some would see me as impetuous
And easily stoked to irrational rage
And others would say I was immovable
Stagnant and set in my ways.

Both would be true
For my impetuosity comes
From being firmly grounded and
My grounding takes shape from
The flashes of inspiration I explore.

I am patient and I am persistent
As I move through life's course
And within my breast beats
A heart that holds the earth's
Wisdom and light deep within.

Taurus is the second sign of the Zodiac and following in the enthusiastic outpour of Aries, Taurus stands ready in its place of a fixed sign. The initial burst of enthusiasm (Aries) is now curbed and brought into form by the concrete solid container that is Taurus. Being a fixed sign, its nature is to hold strong and steady, albeit, immovable at times. This center of the road strength can generate a stable base from which growth of material endeavors flourishes and survives even in the most turbulent of circumstances. The symbol for Taurus is a bull. The choice of this particular animal gives great clue to the innate qualities of Taurus. Strength, sure footedness and earthiness by virtue of its sheer size offer the potential for an individual, who is stalwartly and commanding in their presence.

Taurus is an Earth sign. The energy of Earth is that of fertility, foundation, upholding and the physical and manifest world. In the sign of Taurus, this strength takes the form of stability and a resolute strength that creates the foundation upon which those things of the material world can flourish and grow. Taurus moves effortlessly in all matters of the physical and manifest realm, including business, finances and foundations of home.

Within those who have Taurus as a strong component, there is a predisposition towards a determined attitude and follow through in matters of resolve. Add to this the loyalty to home life and those they are closely connected to. The seemingly obstinate nature of the Taurus energy if well used can be used effectively to ensure that the best outcome will occur. If it is used as a pause to assess in greater detail the situation, take in more information and fully observe before charging ahead, the ultimate goal will be arrived at in a successful and stable manner. Inertia is one of the downfalls of this energy, sometimes waiting too long and allowing stagnation or missing the opportunity to move ahead.

Venus is the Ruling Planet of Taurus. The energy of Venus is that of beauty, harmony and awakening the emotional self. It is the heart that yearns for romance and connection. This energy supports social interaction and the overwhelming goal is to connect at a deep and often intimate level with those of our choosing. A natural love of beauty and great sense of aesthetic style enhance the home life and material endeavors of Taurus.

GEMINI
♊

Mutable - Air

Planetary Ruler - Mercury

Keywords

Duality

Changeability

Communication

Assertiveness

The Power of Polarity, Expression and Intellect
The Path of Adaptability

Arc of Time

Master of illusion
And Mistress of time
I am the mirror reflection
Of that which is reflected
Mind and its gymnastics
Of intellect move at
A speed envied by most.

I am the air that
Moves in form
Of aero-acrobatics.

Seemingly steady and
Straight in course
And then, playing at the
Antics of daredevil who
Dives and peaks in response
To the next intriguing distraction.

Unwavering persistence is not
My natural state
But, the flexibility of
Persistent exploration down paths
Of all manner of endeavor
Is my greatest strength.

For between the pillars of my glyph
Lay the secrets of manifestation.
And the inward arc of line at top and bottom
Are the inpouring of air's inspiration
Reaching as above, so below
Towards the reflection of duality.

Gemini is the third sign of the Zodiac, and completes the triad of the modalities Cardinal to Fixed to Mutable, each flowing into the other. Being of a Mutable Modality, the quality of Gemini is that of flexible expansion. It is this flexibility that offers up the potential for beginnings and endings. This is the ultimate duality that is expressed by the "Twins" of Gemini. Both emanating from one single source, but having split and diverged each expresses it own particular quality of polarity.

If we look at the dynamics of energy thus far, beginning with the cardinal sign of Aries, we could think of the three signs that begin the astrological wheel as the quickening fires (Aries- Fire) within the body of manifestation (Taurus- Earth) that gives rise to aspiring towards the heavens (Gemini- Air). Knowing how each sign moves to the next and the interaction between each as they evolve towards completion (and threshold of renewal) of the wheel in Pisces tells its own unique story of the astrological wheel.

Those born with the sign of Gemini as one of the major three of their chart (Sun, Rising or Moon) have the ability to move quickly and adeptly through any situation. This can also be a detriment, with the details and steps of the process being overlooked. The difficulty in being able to replicate what was created is a by-product of this less than meticulous approach. Communication in all forms is particularly heightened in this astrological sign. Again, with Gemini's nature of duality, the intent can be misunderstood if not clearly thought through and settled on before being expressed.

Gemini is an Air sign. The energy of Air is that of the Mind and the expression of thoughts and ideas through the vehicle of the mental process. Gemini brings this energy to the place of adaptability and having the ability to see both sides of the solution or problem. The downside to this however is potential for indecisiveness and confusion.

Mercury is the Ruling Planet of Gemini and Lord of communication in all of its forms. Speech, art, music, writing, etc. All are held within the energy of Mercury. The infamous effects of a Mercury retrograde speak of failure of technological and human communications. Warnings to read the fine print before signing contracts or entering into agreements and misunderstandings and arguments seem to increase during this time period. This type of activity is an expression of the energy of polarity that is held within Gemini. Negative-positive, male-female, clarity-confusion and all that lay between these extremes are natural expressions of the Gemini mind.

CANCER
♊

Cardinal - Water

Planetary Ruler - Moon

Keywords

Loyalty

Intuitive

Nurturing

Creative

The Power of Intuition, Resourcefulness and Imagination

The Path of Imagination

Those They Hold Dear

By the light of the moon
They move in the thousands
Each intent on its course
Each guided by ancient
Instincts and the call of
The Mother to return home.

The first seeds of yearning
For that which cannot be easily
Revealed and emotions sway to
And fro caught within the
Confines of loyalty and trust.

Dive deep into the murky waters
To retrieve the pearl that is
Perfect and most desired
Reach high towards moon lit
Sky- no task too difficult to
Complete for those you hold dear.

Wait patiently as waters overflow
And memory of treasures long lost
And sentiment lit from the light
Within guides you on your way.

They move by the thousands
Tenacity and determination
The only tool of navigation
And when they reach the water's edge
The union of return to home takes hold
And pulls them closer to those
They hold dear.

Cancer is the fourth sign of the zodiac and is Cardinal in nature. The number four relates to foundations, stability and strength and it is these very attributes in which a Cancer will find their solid ground and comfort zone. Shifting of the sands or waves of turbulent energy, tend to throw them into a state of insecurity. Being a Cardinal sign gives this energy an initial boost, which if in a negative mode will upset the cart, so to speak, with emotional and teary response. If well placed, this initial stream of emotion will find and create its own boundaries of expression and run smoothly and fluidly towards a stable base of loyalty, love and trust.

The energy of Cancer is that of Water or emotion. Its planetary ruler is the Moon which gives clue to the depths and expanse that those whose natal charts hold dominance with Cancer possess. Just as the tides move in a pattern of ebb and flow, so too will the moods and dispositions of those born under the influence of Cancer. The natural tendency is to be a homebody with family being high on the list of priorities in any consideration. Trust and feeling comfortable in a situation are also major considerations when making decisions with the tendency to worry; largely because of the deep emotional connections that Cancer natives tend to make- both to their surroundings and the people who inhabit them.

Those born with the sign of Cancer as one of the major three of their chart (Sun, Rising or Moon) have the ability to not only create the safe and secure environment of family that we crave, but can also be the anchors that weather the storms if they have gained knowledge of their own emotional tides. They nurture and gently guide those they are closest to, being a bit reserved initially with strangers. This is the filter that is used to assess whether they can trust the individual or situation at hand.

The Moon is the Ruling Planet of Cancer so, when the moon's phase is in the sign of Cancer, emotion will run high, the floodgates of intuition will be accessible and opportunities to connect at a deeper level of all interactions and relationships is present. This energy may present in the form of moodiness or withdrawal, primarily with the intent of safe-guarding and filtering the emotional outpour. But if allowed to flourish and move in an unrestricted flow, creative potential and imaginative solutions abound. Just as the moon moves through her phases of darkness and illumination, the native of Cancer will at times reveal their deepest nature for all to see and at others; no one will have a clue as to what is going on with this normally loving and giving person. Allowing them to have their space of retreat and privacy is usually all that is needed to encourage them to move out into the light.

LEO

♌

Fixed - Fire

Planetary Ruler – Sun

Keywords

Action

Authority

Strength

Dynamism

The Power of Generosity, Spontaneity and Leadership
The Path of Self- Expression

The Fire of Will

The light shines fully on my face
And I command attention.

Strong and proud
I will take charge
Where it is needed
And fiercely protect
When challenged unfairly.

My fires and will are constant
And although the spotlight shines
Benevolently on my actions
I often retreat to the coolness
Of shadow when wounded
Or feel vulnerable.

I am Leo
I am the King of the starry
Heavens and beware
The flick of my tail in
Exasperation or the
Ferocity of my roar.

They are but warnings to
Keep your distance
From those people and
Things I nurture and protect.

I stand in rapture as
The flame of sun's rays
Ignites my varied passions.

Resolute will and determination
Guide my unyielding course
As I move with power
And courage to claim
My place of leadership.

Leo is the fifth sign of the Zodiac. Being of a Fixed Modality the quality of Leo is that of stability and unwavering strength. Leo is the Fire that burns steadily urging us onward towards whatever goal has been decided upon, while being ever vigilant in guarding against those energies that would undermine. In the sign of Leo we find the sustaining fuel of our endeavors. Leos, by nature are generally outgoing and find the most comfortable place to be is in the spotlight. If well-aspected, Leos are natural leaders and protectors of what they claim as their own, whether it is relationships, careers, possessions or ideals.

Those born with the sign of Leo as one of the major three of their chart (Sun, Rising or Moon) have an innate ability to lead. They enjoy being in the limelight and take great pride in accomplishment won through effort. Their will is strong and determination underscores all activities. These leadership skills will present in accord with which of the three are being influenced by Leo energy. If the Sun sign is Leo, personalities will be charismatic with a magnetic quality. If the Rising (or ascendant) sign is Leo, their personality will be dynamic and strongly exerted in most situations. And, if Leo is the Moon sign, emotions will be strongly flowing, passionate and willful in nature.

Leo is a Fire sign. The energy of Fire is that of the Action- Will and the desire o be actively engaged in all that is undertaken. Leo brings an intensity to this fiery energy of will that is both strong and supportive. This is the solar power of kingship, authority and strength that magnetically draws to itself a fire of the will.

The Sun is the Ruling Planet of Leo and center of our Heliocentric world. Power, light, heat and sustaining of life are all held within the energy of the Sun. Just as the Sun is the center of our Universe, the energy of Leo is one that enjoys being the center of all activities.

The sun, if you were to get close enough has the maximum pull of magnetic attraction, drawing you into its fiery center, so too, those born with Leo prominent in their chart have an innate quality that attracts attention whether it is driven by curiosity or fueled by notoriety.

Be mindful that the brilliance of charismatic light can be blinding and serve to mask the finer details and subtleties of the Leo person's nature- positive and negative. And just as being too long in the sun can be draining and result in sunburn, the intensity that a strong willed Leo personality exerts can be energy sapping for those of much gentler signs.

Virgo

♍

Mutable - Earth

Planetary Ruler - Mercury

Keywords

Analysis

Refinement

Discrimination

Detail Oriented

The Power of Adaptability, Analysis and Re-formation
The Path of Clarity

Let Me Break it Down

Describe to me again
In detail what it is
That you want me to do.

If you can give me
Sufficient information
I can draw a finely
Tuned conclusion.

But if you omit the
Fine points I will be
Forced to search until I
Have the information I need.

I can be impetuous at times.
And occasionally I appear to be
The neophyte who is thought
To not have nearly enough experience.

These are the qualities that allow
Me to seek and unravel the deepest
Of mysteries I see with the
Eyes of one who has not been
Jaded and corrupted by
Pre-conceived assumptions.

My attention to detail
Is rivaled by none
And my organizational skills
Are something that many
Wish they could master.

I am shrewd and analytical
And will stand strong if
My analytical mind
Is questioned.

Some may see me as
Inert and caught up in the web
Of over-analysis and detail
Others would praise my
Orderly and inquisitive nature.

So next you have need
Of one whose hand
Moves with meticulous grace
Seek me out and let me
Break it down for you.

Virgo is the sixth sign of the Zodiac. Being of a Mutable Earth Modality the quality of Virgo is that of flexible expansion. It is this flexibility that offers up the potential for endings and beginnings. Virgo's gift is the ability to take inventory of what is available as resource, categorize it and then spin it into a useful viable form.

In the process there is a tendency towards tearing down to see what needs to be rebuilt. This is Virgo's style of analysis and sorting or sifting through what will be the most productive course of foundation. This digging down, then digging down again, and then starting the process all over again can lead to no real forward momentum or progress taking place. For those who must work collaboratively with a Virgo, the task can be tedious and appear redundant in nature given the first, second and third iteration of what is a nearly perfected plan of action.

Virgo's zodiacal attribution is the Virgin. When we speak of the virgin regarding the astrological sign it is devoid of its sexual connotation, rather being an expression of one who is not affected nor guided by the physical distractions. In this sense the energy of Virgo is of one who becomes deeply engaged in what the end goal of a project is and is not easily dissuaded, or distracted by limitation, challenge or the naysayers. They take on the goal from a pure and clean perspective.

Those born with the sign of Virgo as one of the major three of their chart (Sun, Rising or Moon) have the ability to reveal the underpinnings of any task they undertake. Relationships become a study in analysis. Jobs become a storehouse of detailed and thoroughly researched outcomes, and personal life is orderly and methodical in its approach. This can also be a detriment, with the attention to detail becoming the primary focus and the conclusive findings held in a state of slow moving stagnation.

Vigo is an Earth sign. The energy of Earth is that of the Physical and manifest world. Virgo takes this fertile ground and pulls from it those weeds that will deter growth and prepares it for receipt of viable seed. The downside to this type of weeding is the tendency, if not kept in check to also disrupt the naturally occurring order of viable matter and rip it from its roots.

Mercury is the Ruling Planet of Virgo and Lord of communication in all of its forms. Its impact on Virgo is that of detail in communication and an analytical style that brings the technical aspect of any endeavor to the surface. Unfortunately, this attention to detail can at times be cumbersome and the more simplistic point that is clamoring to be heard is lost in a sea of, albeit very articulate and thorough red tape.

Libra

♎

Cardinal - Air

Planetary Ruler – Venus

Keywords

Balance

Collaboration

Beauty

Refinement

The Power of Harmony and Teamwork
The Path of Balance

It Is Truly Beautiful

It is truly beautiful!
There is a certain
Refinement and grace.

The craftsmanship is expertise
And one can tell that
Great skill and thought
Went into its creation.

You know, they say
That the finest of gold
Was used and each pan
Was polished and leveled
Its inner workings were
Calibrated to the most
Exact measure.

As I think on it- if, I pause
Too long on either extreme
Of matters the agility of my
Mind usually steps in to set
The course straight and bring
The tangential stream back
To center point.

Although, if I linger too long
In the comfort of my mental
Landscape that brings its own
Downpour of disequilibrium.

Yes, it is beautiful this state
Of affairs and the rarest and
Most refined of thought
Is poised and balanced
On the luminescent
Polished scales of mind's
Elegantly created obelisk.

Libra is the seventh sign of the Zodiac, and is Cardinal Air. Being a Cardinal sign, new ideas and ways of mentally approaching any matter are in keeping with its energy. Libra is the place of balance and weighing the pros and cons of a situation. This is all taken from the perspective of intellectualizing and finding a logical solution that is cooperative and harmonious as well as "appealing". Beauty is a key component here. Not just in the mundane sense but also the quality of beauty that occurs when everything is working as it should in a way that makes sense, is logical and maintains harmony.

Libra is the first of the last six signs of the zodiacal wheel. The qualities that have been present thus far are those of building the personality and learning how to be fully present in that energy. As we move around the wheel and encounter the remaining six signs the emphasis is on outward expression and taking the information that has been gathered thus far and putting it into viable purpose.

Those born with the sign of Libra as one of the major three of their chart (Sun, Rising or Moon) have the ability to use reason and logic as a scale of balance. There is a sense of refinement that infuses everything undertaken and meticulous attention is given to the execution of mental processes, giving the impression that the most complex thought has been easily and delicately arrived at. There can be a sense of coldness or aloofness present in those with Libra prominently in their chart. This stems from wanting balance and harmony and using detachment as the tactic of choice in safeguarding their efforts.

Libra is an Air sign. The energy of Air is that of the Mind and the expression of thoughts and ideas through the vehicle of the mental process. Libra brings this energy to a place of synthesis, eloquence and expression in a way that engages the senses.

Librans are often gifted writers with a beautiful product as the end result. The full process of having the thoughts brought down into a place where it can be expressed in a long- lasting and concrete way is part of the nature of Libra's endeavors towards harmonious beauty.

Venus is the Ruling Planet of Libra. The energy of Venus is that of beauty, harmony and awakening the emotional self. A natural love of beauty and great sense of aesthetic style are enhanced in the energy of Libra. The refinement that is typical of Libran energy is the result of the careful weighing and measuring of all the suitable options. The final choice lies in whichever option will have the most aesthetic impact and appeal. Love, passion and beauty are key words here.

Scorpio

♏

Fixed - Water

Planetary Ruler – Pluto

Keywords

Emotional Power

Introspection

Transformation

Transmutation

The Power of Release, Renewal and Transformation
The Path of Involvement

You Think You Know ME?

You may think that you know Me
But my masks are many and I hide
My secrets well.

My passions are intense and move
Through me flowing like hot lava
Despite my conservative
And cool exterior.

And those of you who think
Me cold and unfeeling

Only see the mastery of my
Facade which protects the exposed
Soft belly beneath.

It is often in the dark of night
That I find the greatest solace
But if I linger too long that place
Of comfort becomes the prison
From which I strain and struggle
To break free.

I pause and breathe deeply
To allow the realization that
These walls of confinement
Are My frightened emotion's
Creation; and the walls crumble
Around me as the light of Dawn
Filters through.

The sands of time shift and flow
From one tightly held container
To another.

The truths of my own history's
Stories are drawn up from the
Darkness and into the blazing sun.
I examine them and relearn
The greater lessons contained
In each.

And, once mastered and reclaimed
As paths back to myself my Spirit soars
And all see me as transformed
The burden has been lifted

And, I look once again towards
The full Light of Day.

No, you will never know
All of my Secrets
Many lay hidden
Buried even to me
But, without their stories
To be lived you would not be
Charmed and seduced by
My enigmatic charisma.

Scorpio is the eighth sign of the Zodiac. The energy of Scorpio is that of Water or emotion. It is the only sign of the Zodiac that has three levels of initiatory experience associated with it. The first is that of the Scorpion; residing unseen and ready to strike if provoked. Its second nature is that of the Eagle who is able to see from great heights and make selection of the smallest of prey while soaring high above. The third attribution of Scorpio is that of the Phoenix. Rising from the ashes of destruction, wings aflame and fully illuminated by the heat of passionate transformative action.

Those born with the sign of Scorpio as one of the major three of their chart (Sun, Rising or Moon) have the ability for deep and powerful work of introspection and self-revelation. If not carefully nurtured, Scorpios can easily fall prey to their baser needs. The same quality that makes for fertile ground for addictions can also be cultivated to be used for potent and transformative shadow work.

Although Scorpio is a water sign; there is an underlying nature of fire held within the scorpion influence. This is the sign of ultimate and permanent transformation. But, beware! Scorpio is also the master of pulling up to the surface those things that lay buried deep within, even if you are not ready for them to be exposed. The resulting benefit can be that of the Phoenix transformed and renewed if you allow Scorpio to do its work.

Pluto is the Ruling Planet of Scorpio. It is the furthest away from Earth and the Sun with very little known of its true nature. This can also be said of the dynamics of Scorpio. Natives of this sign stand in the background silently observing, taking it all in, formulating their opinions and then retreating just as covertly as they arrived. Pluto is the higher vibration of the planet Mars and the assertive energy that is Mars becomes transformed into dynamic and potent powers of persuasion.

Sagittarius

♐

Mutable - Fire

Planetary Ruler – Jupiter

Keywords

Distribution

Outward Reaching

Interconnectedness

Expansion

The Power of Exploration, Initialization and Disbursement

The Path of Distribution

The Hunger

I stand on the horizon- my senses
Keen to the rhythm of life all around me
I breathe in the world's offerings and
Send the experience outward
Always looking towards the sun and sky
And that which is said to be beyond my grasp.

It is this reaching and straining that
Feeds my hunger to explore and extend
Beyond my limitations
And, once my will takes hold

All that lay within my sight
Narrows to a single point of focus.

Restrained tension pulls against
The strength of carefully placed
Goal and the final pause of release
Is that which achieves its apex beyond
The keenest of sight.

Once again, the archer sets the course
As movement becomes dynamic
And primal urge bursts into the flames
Of desire and enthusiasm.

Tension gives way to flexibility of
Intent and directed will issues
Forth from that which has been
Carefully ignited.

I fan the tiny embers
That expand and become
Torches that are held towards
The highest of aspirations
And just as sharpened arrows
Carefully aimed hit the core of
Their determined mark these
Fires I set to burning within you
Will give birth to spontaneity
And finely tempered form.

My paths are many and each is lit
By the embers I have set to
Smoldering deep within.

I am the teacher and the student
Who waits eagerly to blaze a new trail
I am the place from which the Phoenix
Arises and mine is the expanse that
Lights the way as the
Sea goat begins his journey.

Sagittarius is the ninth sign of the Zodiac. The energy of Sagittarius is that of distribution. It is a sign of action. Sagittarius not only walks the path but blazes the trail and lights the way as it moves through new experiences. There is an underlying goal of expanding horizons while remaining within their comfort zone.

Sagittarius is Mutable Fire. Flexible and quantitative in quality, this active principle is expressed as sending out multiple streams of activity in diverse directions and hoping that something will take root. The flexible nature of a mutable sign also gives way to crossing beyond its boundaries and thus releasing what needs to be left behind so the next step towards advancement can be made. In Sagittarius this is typified by the beginning of many new projects, most of which will be left unfinished as desire urges them on towards something new.

Those born with the sign of Sagittarius as one of the major three of their chart (Sun, Rising or Moon) have the ability to inspire enthusiasm for whatever is at hand. There is a subtle magnetic quality about Sagittarius that engages the principle of action in those they encounter. The zodiacal image of Sagittarius is the Archer, and as the Archer they have excellent perception. What is attracted to the Sagittarian is not always what they had as goal at the onset, but the learning process that occurs as they reach out and move in an exploratory way affords them keen perception in their interactions with other people and their needs.

Sagittarius is a Fire sign. The overwhelming energy of Fire is that of transformation through change. It is the fire that sends its sparks out in many directions with the aspirations that one or two will energize, take root and ultimately become the bonfires that quicken and transform. If actively engaged and passionate about whatever change is set into motion the catalytic fires of "will" travel far, fast and wide. Like a brushfire this fast moving energy can raise everything in its path, but if tempered by a strongly framed boundary of Higher Will, the fires will blaze with discernment and affect positive and productive outcome.

Jupiter is the Ruling Planet of Sagittarius. The energy of Jupiter is that of expansion. In its expression through Sagittarius, we find the ultimate networker. This over-reaching quality of extending far and wide is with the intent of covering as much ground as possible so they will be ensured of having at least a few options that are viable. With the multiple paths that the Sagittarian sends out by intent and action and with the energy of Jupiter lending its force to the endeavors there is great potential for moving beyond what was initially thought possible and creating something entirely new carried forward by the intent fueled at its place of origins.

Capricorn

♑

Cardinal - Earth

Planetary Ruler – Saturn

Keywords

Determination

Self-discipline

Contained Exploration

The Power of Discipline, Integrity and Goals

The Path of Commitment

Lens of Sight

Matter of continuum
Depth and breath
Of thin air
One step taken
Carefully and slowly in pace.

Diving deep to feel the
Sting of new beginnings
Structure and form
Taking shape as
Pause recoils.

The Master waits at the
Gate and the Adept
Reaches out gingerly
The hand withdraws.

And the steepness of drop
Reverberates at the base
Of darkened well
Gold coins falling as leaves
Carried within the
Space of airy breath.

Once again, the ascent begins
The space of time claiming
The continuum of earthy
Strength and will.

One step taken
Carefully and slowly in pace.

Capricorn is the tenth sign of the zodiac and its image is that of the sea-goat; equally at home in the depths as well as being able to deftly and precisely scale the steepest cliff. Capricorn's energy lends itself towards being ambitious in nature with a fixed determination to achieve. Because they have often had to climb steep hurtles, once achieving success they are able to use the lessons learned in the ascent to hold them securely at the top.

Those born with the sign of Capricorn as one of the major three of their chart (Sun, Rising or Moon) move slowly and very carefully in their approach, to remain sure-footed and avoid the pitfalls that rushing headlong into endeavors would invite. Because of this methodical approach, there is a longevity and patience that serves them well towards seeing through each endeavor until its conclusion. The unfavorable aspect to this approach is the tendency towards creating unnecessary challenges and road blocks. They do not always see that two paths may be equally safe, albeit one may appear to take the shorter course. The shortcut is often misconstrued as having the greatest risk and so the longer and often more challenging path is undertaken needlessly.

Capricorn is an Earth sign. The quality of earth expressed in Capricorn is strength and agility in navigating the paths of life and material existence, both pleasurable and challenging. They are firmly rooted and anchored in whatever their life's goal becomes and remain steadfast in acquiring the necessary resources to remain solvent and enjoy a comfortable lifestyle.

Saturn is the ruling planet of Capricorn. Saturn is the Lord of Time and the energy of structure as held by the Gates of Time. This gives Capricorn a seemingly expansive perspective on time and using that broad view to set goals and with organized deliberation go about achieving them. There is the feeling that all of time is on their side and they are willing to spend inordinate amounts of time in pursuit of their goals. The additional quality of Saturn is that of regimented structure. This can sometimes lead to having a very narrow perspective about what the best course of action is, but can also serve to bring all the stray bits of resources into a useable well-defined unit.

Aquarius

♒

Fixed – Air
Planetary Ruler – Uranus
Co-Ruler - Saturn

Keywords

Innovation

Individuality

Idealism

Perception

The Power of Vision, Innovation and Focus
The Path of Idealism

The Motherboard

Waters flow within the
Circuitry of electric form
The aperture opens to
Let in more light and
Macrocosm stretches
Beyond the horizon of gaze.

Borne on wings of creative endeavor
And fervor for the unimagined
The space of physical being
Soars above the fields

Of that which is only
Seen by the keenest of eyes.

Fixed and unshakable
The swirlings of mind
Coil out from the lower
Reaches of the Divine
Returning upon themselves
Upwards towards the apex
Of more refined Light.

And, Man in all his
Glory embraces the
Light body of another
Yet to be realized, but is
Seen through the lens
Of the visionary as
The word 'namaste'
Is uttered in the
Sacred Silence.

Aquarius is the eleventh sign of the Zodiac. It is of a Fixed Modality and Air is its element. The Fixed quality that is expressed through Aquarius is that of gathering to itself all manner of information, and then reforming it as a suitable vessel through which an even better stream of information can be disbursed. To say that an Aquarian is innovative only presents the briefest glimpse at the range of skill and adaptable quality of this sign. Being of the quality of mind and intellect, invention and problem solving are the natural gifts of this sign.

Aquarians have an innate ability to see the whole picture of any project. Multiple outcomes and multiple paths to accomplish the finished product are easily formulated and those having Aquarius prominently in their charts are abstract and impactful in their strategies. Because of the abstract nature of their thought processes they are often considered to be eccentric and rebellious. They are neither of these things, simply able to think and see clearly "outside of the box".

Aquarius is the place of the future. The past and/or history of a thing or place does not hold much interest for the Aquarian as they are always looking ahead, and use that as their guiding force in all of their endeavors.

The specific form of Humanitarianism that is often ascribed to the Aquarian is one in which the greater good is always the objective, even if it means the expenditure of a singular one. This ideology gives a first impression of Aquarians being cold and emotionally unattached. Logic precludes emotion and largely the actions taken by an Aquarian are from the perspective of feeling so greatly for right outcome that the detail of explaining the emotional depths of that action are not felt to serve to further the ultimate goal.

Uranus is the ruling planet of Aquarius. Its quality is that of pure energy and catalytic stream that pulses life into everything it encounters. In Aquarius this manifests as having the ability to act as a catalyst to spur humanity on towards its highest expression. Thoughts move through the Aquarian mind like downloads of information, often making it difficult to articulate in an emotional and meaning-filled way. With the energy of Uranus, Aquarius becomes the "Motherboard " of the master computer without whose components the computer would not work nor be able to bring to light the varied forms of communication and information needed for advancement.

Saturn is the co-ruler of Aquarius which brings the dimension of self-discipline and great structure to the energy that Aquarius offers. Saturn's aspect of time gives the overshadowing that in the Aquarian expresses as being conversant of all time-past-present and future- concurrently and in a way that can extract the best and most viable material that is gathered into the next great invention. The regimented approach of Saturn's energy expressed through Aquarius gives the appearance of being unwavering in their stance and opinion and having total disregard for others input. The Aquarian sees this structure as a necessary means towards a goal that is yet unrealized by most.

Pisces
♓

Mutable – Water
Planetary Ruler – Neptune
Co-Ruler - Jupiter

Keywords

Intuition

Compassion

Understanding

Self-transcendence

The Power of Unconditional Love and Flow of Interaction
The Path of Understanding

Seeker Through The Veil

Compassion spills and overflows
The oceans of my Soul
Each drop moving through
Rivulets of prismatic depths.

A cadence of virtuosity as
Fingers move in pizzicato
Rhythm across ephemeral strings
The sounds of empathetic release.

Seeker of that which is
Just beyond the grasp
Slips like sand through
The funnel of glass measured time.

And Devotion pools at the base
Of sun-parched throats
That willingly endure the pain
To spare another the distress.

Martyr and miracle
Saint and sacrifice
Each flow in opposition
Until the water clears
And the darkened path
Of return is revealed
In the depths of mysterious
Waters as compassion
Fills my thirst-quenched
Soul.

Pisces is the twelfth and last sign of the Zodiac. It is the place of having gathered into itself the experience and energy of the previous eleven signs. Just as Aries is the first and initializer of the Wheel, Pisces is the conclusive ending that will eventually expand in a flexible nature and spill forth its emotional outpouring and intuitive wisdom on all who are able to receive. This is the Mutable quality that Pisces uses. That of flexibility – offering up emotional support to any and all – as well as being the bridge towards the catalytic quality of the Cardinal sign of Aries.

Those born with the sign of Pisces as one of the major three of their chart (Sun, Rising or Moon) have an innate ability to heal. They are deeply connected to others of humanity in an emotional way, understanding through feeling and guiding through a love centered approach. Empathetic qualities are abundant in Pisces and natives of this sign will often choose health care oriented professions making excellent care givers, doctors, nurses, etc. Pisceans are giving in a very selfless way, which can also undue their effectiveness as they often neglect their own needs and leave themselves completely depleted, both actively and emotionally.

Pisces is a Water sign. The energy of this type of Water is focused on the emotional and intuitive realms of the individual. We see this clearly exemplified in Pisces as there is great potential for deep insight and connection at an energetic level for those with Pisces prominently in their chart. Additionally, they have deep levels of understanding that serve to support their naturally intuitive nature.

Neptune, is the ruling planet of Pisces and brings with its energy the mystical and dreamy quality that is a natural component in the Pisces attributes. In the study of Esoteric Astrology, Neptune is considered the Higher amplification of Venus. If we consider this thought, Neptune then moves to a place of Higher Love, unconditional compassion and an evolved sense of "beauty" in the world. In the Pisces native "beauty" is highly refined in the sense of seeing the best in each individual, and moreover, feeling that the offering of unconditional Love will change even the worst tendencies in humanity.

Jupiter is the co-ruler of Pisces and is reflected in the over-reaching efforts of the Piscean to heal and offer a helping hand far and wide. So great is their love for humanity and the need to ease human suffering that they will spread themselves thin in the effort and if successful, all lives they touch are that much better for having received this outpouring of genuine and soul-filled caring.

Part Two

Temple of Stars

Astrological Pathworkings

Temple of Stars Pathworkings

How to Use These Pathworkings

There are many ways to imprint the information about each of the astrological signs in your memory. One of the ways that is used in magickal study is through the use of a Pathworking.

Pathworkings differ from guided mediations in that, if skillfully constructed, each component, object, location or color is meant to open your subconscious to a deeper level of understanding. Each word and the way in which you arrive at, leave or interact with a space calls up a stored memory of experience in this or other lifetimes that reveals yet another key to the larger puzzle of our Soul's purpose.

Additionally, these pathworkings can be used to establish a regular meditation practice which will make your mind more receptive to all manner of information and studies.

Good- Read through the pathworking each time you want to use the pathworking. Make note of pausing in the reading wherever it feels like more time would be spent in the specific train of thought.

Better- Read through the pathworking several times and as you do so, try to set up key points that are stored in the memory. In this way, you can create your own scenarios using the structure of the original pathworking without having to read through the text each time.

Best- Employ the physicality of recording the pathworking in your own voice (which produces an effective recognizable neurological imprint inducing physiological response and imprint) to listen to.

When you are ready to make the recording be sure to select a space where you will not be interrupted and has minimal background noise.

Be sure to speak slowly (more so, if you tend to speak quickly and do not annunciate well) and clearly and to give pause where it would naturally occur if you were reading aloud. There may be some points in the meditation where you will want to spend several minutes in the locale that is being presented. Remember to give adequate time of silence for this. Do not stop the recording, pause and restart it. Allow the amount of time you wish to have to fill the space on the recording and then resume the reading of the pathworking.

Regardless of what method you use, remain open and receptive to what presents to you beyond what has been scripted through the pathworking as you move more deeply into this study. Having a journal to record your impressions and keeping record of your progress in memorizing the information and making use of a journal can serve as great encouragement to you. Looking back and seeing how far you have come fuels the desire and gives you markers of growth that are concrete, tangible and acknowledgement of your hard work.

Note: If you wish to use these as meditative tools, use the pathworking appropriate to and for the duration of each sun sign. Do this as a project for the course of a year of solar cycle through each of the astrological signs. Be sure to journal your impressions. Pay particular attention to the period of time that your Natal Sun sign enters and leaves its astrological placement. For example: My natal sun sign is Aquarius. The sun remains in Aquarius from Jan. 20-Feb.18. For the course of this time, I would use the Hall of Aquarius pathworking as my meditative focus. The next sign would be Pisces which would be my focus for the next 29-30 day (approx) period. You will be amazed at what you intuitively learn!

THE HALL OF ARIES

Turn your focus and attention to your breath. Allow the space of your consciousness to move with the rise and fall of your chest and the filling and release of the lungs. Continue in this manner for several breaths; allowing each to become softer, smoother and slower. With each breath your physical body appears to become lighter and your center of consciousness floats upwards towards the inner eye. You feel enveloped by the mist of transition between the Physical and Astral. And as this veil thins you step through a veil of dark blue mist and find yourself standing centrally in a circular room. As you look around you see that this space opens out to a star lit night sky. The velvety blackness above holds a twinkling of starry light that fills the panoramic view above. The walls encircle you and are of a deep bluish purple. As your eyes adjust to this room you notice an archway just ahead of you. It glows a deep blood red in color and you are intrigued by what may lay through the archway.

You step forward and pass easily through the archway stepping through the glyph of Aries and out into a room that is vibrantly colored red. You see the astrological sigil of Aries and feel a surge of youthful exuberant energy wash over you. There is a table placed centrally with a variety of objects placed upon it and you feel the overwhelming desire to explore these items. You gingerly pick up each object, looking carefully at it and seeing that some are similar in use and you begin to create something new that is the summation of what you have selected. You spend some time looking at each object before selecting or discarding it for your final creation. Although many of the objects are commonly found, it is as though you are seeing them for the first time. You feel child-like in wonder and anticipation of what these things will create when put together. Having completed this task, you look around eager for someone to see what you have done. For someone who can take notice of what you have achieved. Disappointed that no one is nearby, you dismantle your project and set to work creating something new. You are sure that this time, someone will appear that you may share this wonderful invention with. As you turn your attention back to your new creation, you hear sounds of laughter coming from the corridor. You look up and see that there are several people entering the room. You are excited to see them, and move towards one of the groups eager to participate and learn who they are and what they are so joyfully discussing. As you approach, one from the group turns towards you and smiles in welcome. She explains that they have just been discussing a new invention and will be giving it a trial run later. You ask them to wait a moment and then quickly retrieve the item you have been creating; ready to proudly show your new invention. Each looks at it and offers some suggestion on improving what you have. You are irritated by this and feel the need to defend the project you have begun. You gather up your will and begin to demonstrate how effectively this object could be used without any improvements. Each nods in agreement as you present your case, not wishing to dampen your enthusiasm. As you become more and more passionate about what great things your new invention can do, the others begin to see more clearly how innovative your approach is. They comment that what you have pointed out about the object were not necessarily of the tried and true mold, but were valid insights. The girl who first smiled at you even suggests that they may be able to make use of some of your active approach in the upcoming presentation of their invention. Encouraged by these words, you place the object back on the work table and begin to describe a new creation that just came to mind. After moving through a few sentences of description, they tell you that it is time for them to leave. That they would love to stay and talk longer, but they must not be late. You exchange good byes, and as they walk away, one of them walks quickly back towards you and tells you that she really enjoyed meeting you and to keep up the good work and fresh approach.

The room returns to the same quiet state that you initially entered and you realize that it is time for you too to return to your routine. You take a final look around, settling your gaze on the object that won you such praise and the items remaining for you to create anew. As you begin to walk back towards the entryway through which you came, you feel abuzz with energy, ideas and enthusiasm about projects yet to be birthed. You feel encouraged and bolstered by the words of praise and proud of the fact that you acted assertively in defense of your creation and turning the group's opinion to one of newer perspective.

As you deepen into these musings, you find that you are once again standing centrally in the circular room. You look upwards towards the night sky and it seems as though a few of the stars are shining a bit more brightly now than when you first entered. You take a deep breath in and as you exhale, you feel enlivened and at peace in this space of celestial beauty. You know you will visit many times again as the solar months progress and the thought fills you with anticipation of what each of your journeys will reveal. You gently close your eyes and when you open them you are surrounded by the blue veil of energy that carried you to this inner sky. As you take a few more deep breaths and fill the intent with awareness of your physical being and return to your physical space, the mist clears and the smells, sounds and sights of the room in which you began our journey floods your senses. You feel the floor beneath you and the chair on which you are sitting. Noises of the mundane world come back filling ear and mind with thoughts of going about the rest of your day or evening. You take a deep breath in, savoring the vestiges of your astral journey and the insight it provided, and strongly exhale out affirming your oneness with the present moment of physical time and space.

THE HALL OF TAURUS

Turn your focus and attention to your breath. Allow the space of your consciousness to move with the rise and fall of your chest and the filling and release of the lungs. Continue in this manner for several breaths; allowing each to become softer, smoother and slower. With each breath your physical body appears to become lighter and your center of consciousness floats upwards towards the inner eye. You feel enveloped by the mist of transition between the Physical and Astral. And as this veil thins you step through a veil of dark blue mist and find yourself standing centrally in a circular room. As you look around you see that this space opens out to a star lit night sky. The velvety blackness above holds a twinkling of starry light that fills the panoramic view above. The walls encircle you and are of a deep bluish purple. As your eyes adjust to this room you notice an archway just ahead of you. It glows a lush green in color and you are intrigued by what may lay through the archway.

As soon as you step into this room you notice the powerful glyph of Taurus. You also notice that it is a bit more difficult to move quickly in this space. It is as though you have become fixed or rooted in the spot on which you are standing and although you wish to move forward there is a bit of hesitancy as you stand your ground. The air has a heavy quality about it, and you surmise that this is more from inertia than density. It takes all your strength and energy to push through this density and you feel as though you are walking on a very windy day facing into the storm. Each step forward increases the feeling of agitation and frustration. Each step forward also makes you step with more grounded effort and with a weightiness of purpose and intent. You feel unyielding in your determination and with slow and steady progress you make your way towards the opposite end of the room. You see just ahead another archway, glowing with an orange hue. You stop for moment and now realize that in your efforts to make your way through this room, you did not take time to look at what may be contained within it.

As you relax into these thoughts, the atmosphere begins to lighten in density. There is a lessening of the pressure that surrounded you and you find you are able to move quite freely now. You look around and see that the room has been decorated with items that instill a sense of family, home and comfort. There are shades of soft earthy greens and reds throughout and the overall quality is one that invites you to linger and relax. The furniture is a bit oversized and would to some be considered bulky, but you find it to be appropriate to the energy of the space. There is an understated opulence about the room and you have a sense that it has been decorated to stimulate all the senses in a very grounded way. You see a wooden desk against one of the walls and see that several piles of folders cover the top. You walk over to it, curious as to what these folders may be. You see that the labels on each refer to very mundane and concrete activities. Finances, home inventory, job search, investment funds and other similar categories hold papers and documents relevant to each. The wall above the desk is decorated with frames that contain pictures of family and children, a beach home and a boat readied for a fishing trip. You surmise that the occupant of this room is very attached to the material world and its offerings and takes great care and effort in organizing and managing to ensure all remains stable and solvent. You also have a sense that this attitude and care is not borne from greed, but more from a practical nature and one of wanting to provide the best and most secure world for those that are loved ones.

As you turn back towards the center of the room, you notice a tall lit curio cabinet just opposite you. You walk towards it and see that there are a variety of small to medium sized glass figurines contained within. Each has been carefully bolstered by stand and/or case to keep the fragile contents from being upset and broken. You also take note that the cabinet itself has been braced clear through with a rod moving from the floor and clean up through the top of the ceiling to hold the cabinet securely and fixed to its spot. This extra effort at securing the contents, cabinet and all, gives rise to your imagining that it would survive just about any form of disruption or turbulence. It is so strongly and securely rooted to its spot, all would remain immovable within the beautifully reflective glass doors. And, those objects that are clearly treasured and perhaps very valuable, even if only from the perspective of the owner, have a loyal and protective caretaker.

As your eyes scan each of the delicately carved figures, you again feel a thickening and density of energy and atmosphere building in the room. You realize that in your musings you have remained inert. In this state of inertia, it is as though the longer you have remained still, the more rooted you have become to this space and the ground beneath you. You notice that the room smells of damp earth and tiny shoots of flower and grass line the edges of the walls. The strength and stability you felt contained with the furnishings has now given way to its manifest expression of fertility and growth. You realize that the care and protection you have seen given to those physical objects can also be harnessed to optimize growth with the natural world and within yourself. Cultivating stability of home, family and finances can be used to ensure the stability of the larger home and family that is earth and all humanity. Prosperity and accumulation of money and financial gain can be used to help the earth and natural world and its inhabitants prosper and draw from its abundance. You stand firmly on the ground beneath you and take in the transformation of this space into that of the natural world clothed in all its strength, stability and beauty. Feelings of love and gratitude flood your being and at this very moment you feel the joy of moving collectively as one- a family enjoying all that the manifest world may offer and fully present in the moment.

As you deepen into these feelings, you close your eyes and breathe deeply drawing in the energy of this space. You take several more breaths and sense that the air about you is lightning and the aroma of earth is fading. You open your eyes and find that you are once again standing centrally in the circular room. You do not remember passing through the archway in which you entered, but realize that you have been standing in a space of fixed strength and great movement. Somehow you have a deep knowing that the return or flow of stability issues forth from this fixed anchor enabling you to move seamlessly and effortlessly in either direction simply by will. You look upwards towards the night sky and it seems as though a few of the stars are shining a bit more brightly now than when you first entered. You take a deep breath in and as you exhale, you feel enlivened and at peace in this space of celestial beauty. You know you will visit many times again as the solar months progress and the thought fills you with anticipation of what each of your journeys will reveal.

You gently close your eyes and when you open them you are surrounded by the blue veil of energy that carried you to this inner sky. As you take a few more deep breaths and fill the intent with awareness of your physical being and return to your physical space, the mist clears and the smells, sounds and sights of the room in which you began our journey floods your senses. You feel the floor beneath you and the chair on which you are sitting. Noises of the mundane world come back filling ear and mind with thoughts of going about the rest of your day or evening. You take a deep breath in, savoring the vestiges of your astral journey and the insight it provided, and strongly exhale out affirming your oneness with the present moment of physical time and space.

THE HALL OF GEMINI

Turn your focus and attention to your breath. Allow the space of your consciousness to move with the rise and fall of your chest and the filling and release of the lungs. Continue in this manner for several breaths; allowing each to become softer, smoother and slower. With each breath your physical body appears to become lighter and your center of consciousness floats upwards towards the inner eye. You feel enveloped by the mist of transition between the Physical and Astral. And as this veil thins you step through a veil of dark blue mist and find yourself standing centrally in a circular room. As you look around you see that this space opens out to a star lit night sky. The velvety blackness above holds a twinkling of starry light that fills the panoramic view above. The walls encircle you and are of a deep bluish purple. As your eyes adjust to this room you notice an archway just ahead of you. The glyph of Gemini, the Twins hovers in the entryway.

As you step through the orange glow of the Glyph of Gemini you see two perfectly mirrored twins sitting having a conversation. They are both blonde and although they appear androgynous, as many children do, there are slight nuances and physical features that separate them as being male and female. They pause in mid-sentence for a moment, turning to acknowledge your arrival, and then turn back to one another continuing the same thread of thought. Question, answer, and statement flash back and forth between the two at lightning speed. You feel both energized and a bit exhausted as your mental processes are not of this mind-set and cannot keep pace with the chameleon like changes in rhythm, clarity and intonation. You turn your attention to the room and see that books line shelves which encompass all four walls; and papers are strewn about haphazardly as though they had recently been impatiently rifled through and then carelessly left wherever they were put. You stand off to the side and observe how each of the children seems to change their mental position at will. One will agree on what statement has been made and then completely disagree about another. The other seeming to mirror every change of its twin with a steady and regulated pace.

They are discussing their favorite activity of reading and as the conversation becomes more excited, they stand and begin to gesture and point to make clearer their statement fact. As they move around the room going from one conversation to another surrounding this book or that you sense that somehow although appearing to be two, they are actually of one mind. That the duality you are seeing is actually the mental acrobatics of a mind that shifts and moves in accord with wherever the stronger enticement lay. This is the secret of their mental agility. The sheer ability to adapt and change at will to suit the needs of the situation. Although you are excited to have solved this one piece of the puzzle and are beginning to feel more at ease in following the direction, speed and flow of their conversation, your attention is drawn to one corner of the room.

You see a beautifully decorated standing mirror placed diagonally in the corner space between two of the walls. As you move towards it, the sound of the conversation seems to fade and just as you come to standing directly in front of the mirror you turn to see if the twins have fallen silent, and see that you are in the room alone. As you turn back towards the mirror you see more clearly your own reflection. You are a bit surprised, because although you recognize the reflection as being yourself, you also notice that there is the slightest bit of difference. It is not something you could concretely describe or even attribute to distortion of the glass; but rather, more of a perception.

Thoughts of the Coney Island fun house mirrors flood your mind, but those are more straightforward in their deception. This is almost transparent in its subtleness. Your eyes focus on the images of the room behind you that are also reflected. And, again the same feeling of something being ever so slightly different bubbles up. As you stand looking at this mirrored image, you notice that your mood has somewhat changed. You had felt energized and excited, but now as you stare into the glass, you feel a heaviness of mind in trying to solve this perplexing state of vision. It seems as though the longer you stare into this reflection, the more withdrawn and irritated you feel. You take a deep breath, sighing heavily. Just as you release the last bit of exhale, you hear the sounds of heated debate and conversation flooding back into the space.

You turn and see that the twins are once again sitting at the table and debating which game is the most challenging. As the sounds become louder, your mood begins to lift as well. You look back at the mirror and are surprised to see that your image, as well as the room behind you are just as you thought they should be. You think on the changeability of perceptions and ideas and how there are always two sides to every process of thought. You think on the flexibility that approach from this aspect permits, but you also remember the sheer exhaustion of that flexibility and the never ending cycle that can be created by not fully committing to one stream of thought.

You look towards the twins once again and see that they too have succumbed to the mental acrobatics. Each rests a blonde curly head on the table-top, eyes closed. You imagine that even in their dreams they are exploring new topics of discussion, new ways of problem solving and always sensing the dual nature of each expression.

As you deepen into these musings, you are surprised to find that you are once again standing centrally in the circular room. You make mental note that there had been no obvious transition from one space to the other and you think back to the trickery of the mirror you gazed into. Giving this no more thought, you look upwards towards the night sky and it seems as though a few of the stars are shining a bit more brightly now than when you first entered. You take a deep breath in and as you exhale, you feel enlivened and at peace in this space of celestial beauty. You know you will visit many times again as the solar months progress and the thought fills you with anticipation of what each of your journeys will reveal. You gently close your eyes and when you open them you are surrounded by the blue veil of energy that carried you to this inner sky. As you take a few more deep breaths and fill the intent with awareness of your physical being and return to your physical space, the mist clears and the smells, sounds and sights of the room in which you began our journey floods your senses. You feel the floor beneath you and the chair on which you are sitting. Noises of the mundane world come back filling ear and mind with thoughts of going about the rest of your day or evening. You take a deep breath in, savoring the vestiges of your astral journey and the insight it provided, and strongly exhale out affirming your oneness with the present moment of physical time and space.

THE HALL OF CANCER

Turn your focus and attention to your breath. Allow the space of your consciousness to move with the rise and fall of your chest and the filling and release of the lungs. Continue in this manner for several breaths; allowing each to become softer, smoother and slower. With each breath your physical body appears to become lighter and your center of consciousness floats upwards towards the inner eye. You feel enveloped by the mist of transition between the Physical and Astral. And as this veil thins you step through a veil of dark blue mist and find yourself standing centrally in a circular room. As you look around you see that this space opens out to a star lit night sky. The velvety blackness above holds a twinkling of starry light that fills the panoramic view above. The walls encircle you and are of a deep bluish purple. As your eyes adjust to this room you notice an archway just ahead of you. The glyph of Cancer, the Crab hovers in the entryway, seeming to glow from an innermost light.

As soon as you step through the archway and the luminous white glow of the Glyph of Cancer the smells of the ocean and its waters permeate your senses. The fullness of moonlight reflects back from water's edge and there is a sense of stillness and anticipation as the waves gently crest and fall. You feel alive and connected to everything. Your senses are alive with sounds and sights that come in flashes of liquid and heart filled memory. Emotion wells up deep inside of you and the beauty and serenity of this place seems almost more than you can bear. You pause for a moment regaining your composure and take a deep full breath to calm the rising emotions. The scene before you moves you to think back on vacations spent with family and friends at the beach. Cool nights walking barefoot in the moonlight and seeing the familiar and welcoming lights of your summer home. The sounds of laughter spilling like music across the beach and the security and sense of belonging that you so finely crafted within your home.

Feeling content and wanting to spend a bit of time alone, you sit on the cool sand and look out at the moonlit ocean. You feel safe and calm in this setting; almost as though this was precisely the place of energy and state of being that is required to feed and nurture your feeling nature. The sound of the water lapping at the sandy shore creates a mesmerizing and calming feeling within you and scenes of your past experiences pass easily and gently as you close your eyes and relax into the inner screen of your awareness.

You see yourself at the time of meeting your now best friend. You remember the feeling of hesitancy and an awkward shyness at first.

This is what you usually feel at first meetings; a little vulnerable and hesitant to share your deep feeling nature. Your friend sensed this reserve and persevered in trying to get to know you and before you knew it trust had been won and you felt at home and at ease sharing your most private thoughts and feelings with this person. Your friend said you were the most loyal and nurturing person they had ever met and that you made them feel more like family than just friends. And, although there were rocky times you have remained loyal and committed to the emotional bond the two of you have. The memories of this time and the longstanding friendship and shared experiences have been deeply treasured.

You also think on a time when you felt so overwhelmed by worry that you retreated for days into your own little world. The normal calm state and kind words that you eagerly shared became sullen answers and silence. This was your mechanism for protecting the vulnerability you felt. You remember the discomfort you felt at reacting this way, wanting to reach out and nurture and heal those around you, but feeling as though there was simply too much to be felt and not enough of you to help relieve the burden of it.

You realize as you think on these two counterpoints how similar they are to the ebb and flow of the waters a few feet away from where you are sitting. The flexibility and sometimes giving fully and at other times retreating back to the larger source for renewal and replenishment are your natural state. Emotions are the waters within you that if they remained never changing would stagnate and dry up. There would be no source to feed the mental processes and no waters of inspiration to draw upon when you are in your most intuitive and creative state. As these last thoughts slowly and fully pass through you a gentle pulse of water brushes the tips of your toes resting on the now damp sand. The tide is coming in and in your reveries you did not notice the movement towards you. It is a reminder to you to remain fully present, even in your place of introspection. That your emotions can be used to inform and to bring you closer to the serenity of the moment, without having to overcome and overwhelm you.

You stand and breathe in the fresh salty air. You look up towards the fullness of the moon and once again the feeling of safeness and home permeates and floods through you. You look back towards your house and see that the lights have been dimmed a bit and a warm glow shines from each of the windows. Inside are those you love. And, in the cycle of return you feel their love for you. Your best friend has come to visit for the weekend, as well, and you now see someone approaching from the house and calling out to you to come in for a game of scrabble and cup of warm tea. Feelings of gratitude and great care for those in your life fills you and you take one last look at the expanse of ocean.

As you begin to walk towards your friend to answer the call the images slowly fade with each step until once again you find that you are standing centrally in the circular room. You look upwards towards the night sky and see the full moon shining brightly into the Hall. You take a deep breath in and as you exhale, you feel enlivened and at peace in this space of celestial beauty. You know you will visit many times again as the solar months progress and the thought fills you with anticipation of what each of your journeys will reveal. You gently close your eyes and when you open them you are surrounded by the blue veil of energy that carried you to this inner sky. As you take a few more deep breaths and fill the intent with awareness of your physical being and return to your physical space, the mist clears and the smells, sounds and sights of the room in which you began our journey floods your senses. You feel the floor beneath you and the chair on which you are sitting. Noises of the mundane world come back filling ear and mind with thoughts of going about the rest of your day or evening. You take a deep breath in, savoring the vestiges of your astral journey and the insight it provided, and strongly exhale out affirming your oneness with the present moment of physical time and space.

THE HALL OF LEO

Turn your focus and attention to your breath. Allow the space of your consciousness to move with the rise and fall of your chest and the filling and release of the lungs. Continue in this manner for several breaths; allowing each to become softer, smoother and slower. With each breath your physical body appears to become lighter and your center of consciousness floats upwards towards the inner eye. You feel enveloped by the mist of transition between the Physical and Astral. And as this veil thins you step through a veil of dark blue mist and find yourself standing centrally in a circular room. As you look around you see that this space opens out to a star lit night sky. The velvety blackness above holds a twinkling of starry light that fills the panoramic view above. The walls encircle you and are of a deep bluish purple. As your eyes adjust to this room you notice an archway just ahead of you. The glyph of Leo, the Lion hovers in the entryway.

Passing through the glyph, there is an intensity of sudden heat and you find that you are standing on a desert that is scorched and parched from the heat of the Sun. Every direction you look in stretches beyond your end of sight; albeit illuminated in flashes of brilliance of light randomly interspersed throughout the landscape. In the distance you hear the low rumble of what may hold promise of a much needed thunderstorm and the strength that you feel in this place increases as the sun rises higher in the sky. You take some time to languish in this sensation of commanding all that you see.

You feel as though you are the center of this world and there is nothing that you could not accomplish. All of your strengths and weaknesses are lit by the rays of the sun, leaving no facet of your being hidden. It is as though you are standing center stage with the spotlight aimed directly at you and all await the brilliance of your performance. This generates an exuberance and feeling of confidence that is grounded deep within your core of center.

The fires of passion fill your belly with desire to create, to protect and to guard well those you love. There is a primal ferocity to this feeling that you have never experienced before and you know that you would travel to the ends of the earth to safeguard those you hold dear to you. You think on your family and those you have responsibility for and in response to this feeling, you let out a loud and deep guttural sound that comes from a place deep inside and contains more strength and courage than you imagined could be possible. The sound carries into the distance and across this wasteland and you feel in control and powerful.

You stand strong and centered in your own power. You look out surveying all that lay ahead as though this place is your kingdom and all who enter are at your mercy in accord with their own actions. You look upwards and take in the light of the Sun and feel attuned to its life-giving energy. You think on the place of your own inner Sun and the ability you have to bring it to a place of brilliance fueled by your inner passions and desires and bolstered by your will and courage of Heart. You promise yourself that you will act upon these feelings and thoughts to safeguard all you encounter.

As you deepen into these musings, you find that you are once again standing centrally in the circular room. You look upwards towards the night sky and it seems as though a few of the stars are shining a bit more brightly now than when you first entered. You take a deep breath in and as you exhale, you feel enlivened and at peace in this space of celestial beauty. You know you will visit many times again as the solar months progress and the thought fills you with anticipation of what each of your journeys will reveal.

You gently close your eyes and when you open them you are surrounded by the blue veil of energy that carried you to this inner sky. As you take a few more deep breaths and fill the intent with awareness of your physical being and return to your physical space, the mist clears and the smells, sounds and sights of the room in which you began our journey floods your senses. You feel the floor beneath you and the chair on which you are sitting. Noises of the mundane world come back filling ear and mind with thoughts of going about the rest of your day or evening. You take a deep breath in, savoring the vestiges of your astral journey and the insight it provided, and strongly exhale out affirming your oneness with the present moment of physical time and space.

THE HALL OF VIRGO

Turn your focus and attention to your breath. Allow the space of your consciousness to move with the rise and fall of your chest and the filling and release of the lungs. Continue in this manner for several breaths; allowing each to become softer, smoother and slower. With each breath your physical body appears to become lighter and your center of consciousness floats upwards towards the inner eye. You feel enveloped by the mist of transition between the Physical and Astral. And as this veil thins you step through a veil of dark blue mist and find yourself standing centrally in a circular room. As you look around you see that this space opens out to a star lit night sky. The velvety blackness above holds a twinkling of starry light that fills the panoramic view above. The walls encircle you and are of a deep bluish purple. As your eyes adjust to this

room you notice an archway just ahead of you. The glyph of Virgo, the Virgin hovers in the entryway.

As you move forward through the glyph of Virgo you step into an earth-toned room that has newly polished file cabinets lining the walls. Everything is placed neatly and precisely organized. There is a sense of great detail in all that you see. Everything is labeled and you have the sense that nothing is out of place. There is a very grounded feeling about this space; the richly grained woods and colors make you feel at ease.

You are immediately greeted by a lithe beautiful woman whose age is difficult to tell, and with a gentle persuasive voice she asks that you take a seat at her desk on one of the polished wooden chairs. Once sitting, she asks that you describe in detail the experience of your journey thus far. As you begin to recount your story, she takes notes on several pages of a large legal pad, each stroke of pen seeming to coincide and give added emphasis to the words you are saying. Each sentence you relate prompts a question from her and you realize that in this way, she is helping you remember and tell your story with far more detail and accuracy than you would have. Page after page is filled and you find it interesting that you have this much information to share.

It seems as though you and she work in this way for hours and you are surprised to find that only an hour and a half has passed since you first arrived. You finish the last bit of your story and she writes the final sentences down on her pad. She looks up at you with deep penetrating eyes and gently speaks, promising to review the notes later, check them for accuracy and bind them in a richly detailed journal for you to pick up in a few days. You feel comfortable in this place and would like to stay longer, but you are excited about beginning another journey and having that recorded as well. As you rise to leave, she extends a neatly manicured hand and you seal the exchange with a handshake. You turn to go and gently close your eyes and when you open them you are surrounded by the blue veil of energy that carried you to this inner sky. As you take a few more deep breaths and fill the intent with awareness of your physical being and return to your physical space, the mist clears and the smells, sounds and sights of the room in which you began our journey floods your senses. You feel the floor beneath you and the chair on which you are sitting. Noises of the mundane world come back filling ear and mind with thoughts of going about the rest of your day or evening. You take a deep breath in, savoring the vestiges of your astral journey and the insight it provided, and strongly exhale out affirming your oneness with the present moment of physical time and space.

THE HALL OF LIBRA

Turn your focus and attention to your breath. Allow the space of your consciousness to move with the rise and fall of your chest and the filling and release of the lungs. Continue in this manner for several breaths; allowing each to become softer, smoother and slower. With each breath your physical body appears to become lighter and your center of consciousness floats upwards towards the inner eye. You feel enveloped by the mist of transition between the Physical and Astral. And as this veil thins you step through a veil of dark blue mist and find yourself standing centrally in a circular room. As you look around you see that this space opens out to a star lit night sky. The velvety blackness above holds a twinkling of starry light that fills the panoramic view above. The walls encircle you and are of a deep bluish purple. As your eyes adjust to this room you notice an archway just ahead of you. The glyph of Libra, the Scales hovers in the entryway.

You step through the glyph of Libra into an ornate and richly decorated room filled with gold and gemstones. Surrounding you are workbenches and expert jewelers and metal smiths crafting rings. The gold is measured precisely on scales that gleam and balance with the slightest breath of touch, and after careful weighing and scrutiny for imperfection, it is melted into a liquid spun of light and heat. As the mold is filled with this refined essence, gems of varying shapes and sizes are inspected and one, a rare and perfectly faceted emerald, is selected to be the main focus of the piece of jewelry.

As you look around, you notice artwork that is beautiful and insightful on each of the walls. Each brush stroke appears to have been precisely placed and the spectrum of color vibrates in intensity and hue. Each painting has been hung with just the correct amount of lighting and the pieces of sculpture are placed in a pattern that is aesthetically pleasing and functional.

You step through a doorway and into another room where shelves of books line the walls and you have the sense that each has been carefully selected and placed adjacent to a corresponding title that would enhance the readers' pleasure. This room smells of fine leather binding and ink on pages of delicately crafted paper. The librarians move quietly around this space, each collaborating with another before placing a book just so. Everything is very peaceful and those sitting at luxurious wooden reading tables have an expression of contentment on their faces. You are surrounded by luxury, beauty and harmony of mind and heart. You step over to one of the bookshelves and reach towards a beautifully leather bound edition of Leo Tolstoy's *Anna Karenina*. You leaf through the pages and decide that you are not in the frame of mind right now to beginning reading such a weighty tome. You place the book back on the shelf and as quickly as its edges skim the shelf's edge there is a pause in the energy of the room. One of the librarians moves towards you and those at the reading table look up from their books as though disturbed by an annoying sound.

A slender hand reaches out and quickly plucks the book from your hand and places it just a few books away on another part of the same shelf. She quietly informs you that each book has its own spot on the shelf. Each holds its own particular place in the larger organization of the books lining the shelves. She continues to explain that although all the books are not the same size, shape or weight, each is important to the overall balance and aesthetic visual quality that displays order, well planned thought and precise action. She then turns and walks back to the project she was engaged in before the disequilibrium of your misplacing the book.

You are neither offended nor apathetic about the exchange that just took place. You understand the need for that type of balance and order and appreciate the refined and gentle way in which you were corrected about your action. You step through the doorway and reenter the space of artisans and jewelry makers and think about how they too have a certain order they must follow. Each component in the paintings may not be of equal measure, but together they form a beautiful image.

You pause as you look around and muse a little more deeply on this concept. This is not a place that is easy to leave but as you stand in the midst of all of this beauty a feeling of sadness wells up within you. You realize that this opulence is not the normal standard for most. That beauty this rare is not often enjoyed by those of limited means. You see an underlying and certain darkness about this place and as the brilliance of gold and gem dims you notice the vastness of this space.

You turn and take in this sight one last time and gently close your eyes and when you open them you are surrounded by the blue veil of energy that carried you to this inner sky. As you take a few more deep breaths and fill the intent with awareness of your physical being and return to your physical space, the mist clears and the smells, sounds and sights of the room in which you began our journey floods your senses. You feel the floor beneath you and the chair on which you are sitting. Noises of the mundane world come back filling ear and mind with thoughts of going about the rest of your day or evening. You take a deep breath in, savoring the vestiges of your astral journey and the insight it provided, and strongly exhale out affirming your oneness with the present moment of physical time and space.

THE HALL OF SCORPIO

Turn your focus and attention to your breath. Allow the space of your consciousness to move with the rise and fall of your chest and the filling and release of the lungs. Continue in this manner for several breaths; allowing each to become softer, smoother and slower. With each breath your physical body appears to become lighter and your center of consciousness floats upwards towards the inner eye. You feel enveloped by the mist of transition between the Physical and Astral. And as this veil thins you step through a veil of dark blue mist and find yourself standing centrally in a circular room. As you look around you see that this space opens out to a star lit night sky. The velvety blackness above holds a twinkling of starry light that fills the panoramic view above. The walls encircle you and are of a deep bluish purple. As your eyes adjust to this room you notice an archway just ahead of you. The glyph of Scorpio, the Scorpion hovers in the entryway.

As soon as you pass through the glyph of Scorpio you are engulfed in shadow. Glimpses of light are hidden beneath what appear to be shadowy figures and although you do not feel threatened, you know this is a place of great power and well deserving of care and respect as you pass through. There are smells of dampness and decay and you surmise that you are underground. The ground underfoot is solid dirt and you are aware of the hidden and diverse life that this space holds. You stretch a hand out to the side and your fingers brush against a cool damp stone wall and you sense the ceiling of this space is stone as well and not very high above your head. The impression is one of being enclosed tightly in a very confining space.

You move forward as your eyes become adjusted to the darkness and take note that in contrast to your original impression this seems to be a large open cavernous space. Even in the darkness you can discern recesses at various points in the space , although you are not sure that they lead to any other paths.

You pause for a moment and turn towards your right and see that one of the walls appears to be sparkling with random flecks of shadowy light. You step towards it and are surprised to see that a full length mirror is embedded in the smooth stone. Although you wish to leave this place as quickly as possible, curiosity takes hold and you cannot resist the temptation to glance into the mirror ever so briefly.

As you move with trepidation closer towards it, all manner of thoughts and emotions rise up from a place deep within your core. You feel a magnetic pull deep within that seems to be connecting you to what image may be seen in this reflective surface. It is as though you have a great secret that you are excited about, yet unwilling to share with anyone else for fear of what the response may be. You move your head forward so you can get a better look and stare deeply into the reflection in the mirror.

You see the shadowy outline of what you think is your own form, but it seems to shift and change ever so slightly, almost imperceptibly, although you are not moving. You take a deep breath in and close your eyes briefly hoping that when you open them the image will appear more clearly. As you open your eyes you now are able to clearly see the reflection of your own face. You look deeply at this image and the emotions within you begin to well up in response to what you see.

Although the image is recognizable as yourself, there is something a bit askew with the image; a bit disconcerting and similar in expression to what you have seen on others when they had something they wished not to share. These thoughts trigger other emotions within you and you think back on each time you have not been forthright in your dealings or had a harsh word to say when you should have held your tongue.

Each emotion, each deeply buried thought seems to appear etched on your face, held in the stance of your posture and staring back at you. Some are things you thought you had released long ago and others are newly formed. You know that even though this experience is uncomfortable it is necessary and will bring to light the best of your nature through the harsh fires of your own self-awareness and brutal scrutiny.

You are at once mesmerized and repulsed by all that you see and when you have seen as much as you can bear at this time, you feel the urge to recoil and turn away from the harshness of this new reality. You decide to take a few steps backing away from the images and with each step you feel lighter and clearer, unburdened by your secrets and notice that all of your senses are acutely heightened. Your image has changed now as well and there is a soft shade of light framing you; the edges gently feathered in appearance. It glows a gentle reddish orange, like the afterglow of a blazing fire and you feel uplifted and free. You turn away from the mirror and see that the glow is coming from an opening just above you. It is the softness of the morning sun as it rises and the rays of light are now streaming down into the dark cavernous space in which you stand. You feel warmed and enlivened and as though newly reborn.

As the energy of hope and renewal flow through you, you gently close your eyes and when you open them you are surrounded by the blue veil of energy that carried you to this inner sky. As you take a few more deep breaths and fill the intent with awareness of your physical being and return to your physical space, the mist clears and the smells, sounds and sights of the room in which you began our journey floods your senses. You feel the floor beneath you and the chair on which you are sitting. Noises of the mundane world come back filling ear and mind with thoughts of going about the rest of your day or evening. You take a deep breath in, savoring the vestiges of your astral journey and the insight it provided, and strongly exhale out affirming your oneness with the present moment of physical time and space.

THE HALL OF SAGITTARIUS

Turn your focus and attention to your breath. Allow the space of your consciousness to move with the rise and fall of your chest and the filling and release of the lungs. Continue in this manner for several breaths; allowing each to become softer, smoother and slower. With each breath your physical body appears to become lighter and your center of consciousness floats upwards towards the inner eye. You feel enveloped by the mist of transition between the Physical and Astral. And as this veil thins you step through a veil of dark blue mist and find yourself standing centrally in a circular room. As you look around you see that this space opens out to a star lit night sky. The velvety blackness above holds a twinkling of starry light that fills the panoramic view above. The walls encircle you and are of a deep bluish purple. As your eyes adjust to this

room you notice an archway just ahead of you. The glyph of Sagittarius, the Archer hovers in the entryway.

You pass easily through the glyph of Sagittarius. Little sparks of flame lay at your feet creating a pathway through which you begin to walk. You look down and get a bit closer to one and notice that from each of the sparks a single flower appears to be in the process of blooming. As you look more closely, inspecting each along the path you see that some are viable and some wither and die as the spark goes out. Some appear to be desperately trying to take root and others never seem to catch on at all.

You think on the image of the archer, bursting with enthusiasm at the promise of hitting the center mark. The strain of arrow pressed back against bending bow and the sigh of release and effort as it is sent towards its destination. The energy of enthusiasm that turns to disappointment at those arrows shot in vain and then turning to pride in accomplishment at those that hit the target fills this space. You remind yourself that a sharp eye and a steady hand can be the detriment or the success of your endeavors.

You continue moving along the path and as you look deeply at each of these tiny flames you are reminded of the many times you have exerted your will in disbursed effort and the outcomes of those tiny flames of action you set forth. You think on all the experiences you have been afforded by putting your intent out into the greater world, and how those successes and failures have shaped and transformed who you are now.

Your attention is drawn to the sound of something crackling just off the path you are walking upon; and the smell of wood burning wafts thick in the air. You turn in the direction of where the sound seems to be coming from, your pace quickening till you find that you are now running fueled by enthusiasm and excitement about what you may find. You realize you have run nearly to the end of this uncleared passage your aim clear and true.

You stop suddenly and find yourself in a clearing, a bonfire raging hot and colorful just ahead. No one else is around and it is untended, although appearing to be perfectly controlled. As you walk closer you can feel its heat and the sheer beauty of its flames reaching upwards sends shivers of excitement running through you. You look down at your feet and see that the field is covered in the tiny flowers you saw on the main path held within the tiny embers of flame. They form intricate and diverse meandering patterns, but all coil in to the central bonfire. All feeding into its mass.

You realize that these are the arrows of thought, idea and action that are released with intent and purpose. You now understand the necessity for many options to be offered up before one or two can actually ignite what will blaze longer and with more intensity than expected. The one successful endeavor is fueled by the will and desires of many. You take in the smell of the fire as it burns; the depth of multiple colors dancing within its flames and the sound of crackling and the hiss of release.

You deepen into these sensations and you gently close your eyes and when you open them you are surrounded by the blue veil of energy that carried you to this inner sky. As you take a few more deep breaths and fill the intent with awareness of your physical being and return to your physical space, the mist clears and the smells, sounds and sights of the room in which you began our journey floods your senses. You feel the floor beneath you and the chair on which you are sitting. Noises of the mundane world come back filling ear and mind with thoughts of going about the rest of your day or evening. You take a deep breath in, savoring the vestiges of your astral journey and the insight it provided, and strongly exhale out affirming your oneness with the present moment of physical time and space.

THE HALL OF CAPRICORN

Turn your focus and attention to your breath. Allow the space of your consciousness to move with the rise and fall of your chest and the filling and release of the lungs. Continue in this manner for several breaths; allowing each to become softer, smoother and slower. With each breath your physical body appears to become lighter and your center of consciousness floats upwards towards the inner eye. You feel enveloped by the mist of transition between the Physical and Astral. And as this veil thins you step through a veil of dark blue mist and find yourself standing centrally in a circular room. As you look around you see that this space opens out to a star lit night sky. The velvety blackness above holds a twinkling of starry light that fills the panoramic view above. The walls encircle you and are of a deep bluish purple. As your eyes adjust to this room you notice an archway just ahead of you. The glyph of Capricorn, the Sea-Goat hovers in the entryway.

You cross through the entryway and appear to be walking towards absolute darkness. You take a few steps forward and find yourself standing at the edge of a cliff. It is evening and the darkness you saw was the velvety blackness of sky. You look downwards and see a sheer drop, very steep and not likely to be navigated in this darkness. You stand steady and still, contemplating if you should turn and go back and no sooner has that thought reached its end than a flash of brilliance lights up the night sky. You are unsure of the source, and turn to look behind you and look upwards to see that the light appears to be coming from a ledge a little further above you. It is steady and growing in brightness. Your goal now is to reach that light as the place on which you are standing has darkened considerably and now feels very narrow and unstable.

As you move closer to the wall that you must scale to reach the ledge above you see that this ledge connects just a short distance across to another mountain directly opposite you. You had not noticed this other mountain when you first stepped out through the entryway, and question if it was even there originally, or somehow has just appeared. You calculate in your mind that if you could reach that top ledge you could pass safely to the other mountain which seems to slope gently out towards open ground. You approach the wall and begin to climb steadily up the side towards a small opening in the stone that leads out to the connecting ledge. You realize that this side of the mountain is not as steep as you thought and there are enough small crevices in the solid rock to maintain a strong hand and foot hold.

You extend each arm, reaching upwards with all your might and are determined to accomplish this task. Each movement seems to come more easily as the determination becomes resolve. With continuous upward momentum, you finally pull yourself up and through the opening and come to rest on the connecting ledge. You look out from this elevated view and you feel as though you are standing at the top of the world. Looking down towards the ledge you just came from, you see that the distance you scaled was far higher and steeper than it appeared initially or as you were climbing. Feelings of pride at your success well up inside; you feel strong grounded and powerful. You rest for a moment, breathing deeply from the exertion and taking time to assess what the next course of action should be. You can see that this connecting ledge it is wide enough for safe passage walking and there is indeed an opening in the rock offering entry to the second mountain. You continue sitting for a moment and breathe deeply, reaffirming your pride in the effort and your achievement. You feel energized and alive and no longer feel the need to reach the other side. You have conquered this mountain and moved with surefootedness, good judgment and purpose, which for now is all that is needed.

You allow the joy of these thoughts to move through you and gently close your eyes. When you open them you are surrounded by the blue veil of energy that carried you to this inner sky. As you take a few more deep breaths and fill the intent with awareness of your physical being and return to your physical space, the mist clears and the smells, sounds and sights of the room in which you began our journey floods your senses. You feel the floor beneath you and the chair on which you are sitting. Noises of the mundane world come back filling ear and mind with thoughts of going about the rest of your day or evening. You take a deep breath in, savoring the vestiges of your astral journey and the insight it provided, and strongly exhale out affirming your oneness with the present moment of physical time and space.

THE HALL OF AQUARIUS

Turn your focus and attention to your breath. Allow the space of your consciousness to move with the rise and fall of your chest and the filling and release of the lungs. Continue in this manner for several breaths; allowing each to become softer, smoother and slower. With each breath your physical body appears to become lighter and your center of consciousness floats upwards towards the inner eye. You feel enveloped by the mist of transition between the Physical and Astral. And as this veil thins you step through a veil of dark blue mist and find yourself standing centrally in a circular room. As you look around you see that this space opens out to a star lit night sky. The velvety blackness above holds a twinkling of starry light that fills the panoramic view above. The walls encircle you and are of a deep bluish purple. As your eyes adjust to this

room you notice an archway just ahead of you. The glyph of Aquarius, the Water Bearer hovers in the entryway.

Immediately, as you step into the room you feel alive with energy. The air is pulsing with it and cobalt blue and white strands of lightning like currents run down the sides of the walls. You feel inspired and enlivened and all manner of invention and idea comes rushing into your mind for your consideration. It is as though you can see everything from a greater perspective.

Your thoughts move with a speed and clarity of focus and intent that to many would be exhausting, but in this space of energy that is the core essence of the electric mind's nature. It is as though you are receiving multiple downloads of information, simultaneously and are able to decipher, categorize, recombine and formulate an accurate and useful conclusion in the space of a single breath.

You turn your thoughts to the natural world; its challenges and threat to its future. The depths of the ocean and its life fill your vision. Each particle of life held within its watery realm appears as strands and streams of electrified light and energy. The solution to restoring the waters to healthy condition is clearly laid out and you see the successful end result of taking action. The canopies of the rainforest and somehow all the life that is hidden form normal sight are now revealed as though soaring above with the keen eyesight of the hawk. Each tree and leaf, insect and animal become points of light on an unending webbing that expands and encompasses everything around it. You see the tragic outcome if this webbing and connection is shattered and unraveled and you see exactly and precisely what must be sacrificed to ensure that the greater webbing will survive.

You see the entire Planet and its inhabitants and the vital role each and every thing plays in sustaining the greater cosmic cycles and flow. You see the world and the Universe with fresh understanding and are optimistic about the future that could be. You see everyone and everything as part of the greater whole and now have a renewed sense of how that whole may be served and of what actions must be taken towards a future that sees life as a unified process.

As you are processing all of these new experiences a feeling of great compassion and love engulfs you. Your forward thinking energy has moved you towards the next turn of the Wheel and you envision the glyph of Pisces and know that this is what is calling forth your humane and compassionate self. You realize that the brilliance of mind is unproductive, dimmed and lack luster without the compassion of heart.

You gently close your eyes and when you open them you are surrounded by the blue veil of energy that carried you to this inner sky. As you take a few more deep breaths and fill the intent with awareness of your physical being and return to your physical space, the mist clears and the smells, sounds and sights of the room in which you began our journey floods your senses. You feel the floor beneath you and the chair on which you are sitting. Noises of the mundane world come back filling ear and mind with thoughts of going about the rest of your day or evening. You take a deep breath in, savoring the vestiges of your astral journey and the insight it provided, and strongly exhale out affirming your oneness with the present moment of physical time and space.

THE HALL OF PISCES

Turn your focus and attention to your breath. Allow the space of your consciousness to move with the rise and fall of your chest and the filling and release of the lungs. Continue in this manner for several breaths; allowing each to become softer, smoother and slower. With each breath your physical body appears to become lighter and your center of consciousness floats upwards towards the inner eye. You feel enveloped by the mist of transition between the Physical and Astral. And as this veil thins you step through a veil of dark blue mist and find yourself standing centrally in a circular room. As you look around you see that this space opens out to a star lit night sky. The velvety blackness above holds a twinkling of starry light that fills the panoramic view above. The walls encircle you and are of a deep bluish purple. As your eyes adjust to this room you notice an archway just ahead of you. The glyph of Pisces, the Fish hovers in the entryway.

There is an iridescent turquoise shimmer about the glyph of Pisces and as you step through the archway you are aware of being somehow underwater, yet able to breathe normally. You hear the cries of the whales in the distance and look upon the varied sea life that surrounds you. You take note that although you can see shapes and form, they are distorted and the murkiness of the water seems to cast shadows in an undulating, rhythmical manner. You feel the pressure of the water on your body and yet also have the feeling of weightlessness. It is as though you are gently being upheld and carried by something that is intangible and invisible yet powerful in its depth and density.

You look up and see the faint glimmer of light above you creating a kaleidoscope of patterns and extending both arms upward feel yourself being lifted towards what appears to the surface of the waters. Fingers extend through the top of a gently cresting wave and you emerge from the depths looking upon a sandy shore just ahead of you. You feel soft sand beneath your feet and stand up, stepping out onto warm soft gray sand.

You look around and see that the beach stretches endlessly ahead and you are alone in this place of earth and water. It feels as though you have emerged at the very end of the earth and you have a sense that there are many stories and much wisdom held in the expanse of this place. As you reflect on these thoughts you take a few steps forward and pause for a moment, now becoming aware of a formless shape several feet ahead of you.

As you move closer you see that this form is that of half fish and half woman. You move around her for a closer look and she lifts her head revealing beautiful eyes that are the color of the clearest bluest ocean waters. As you look deeply into her eyes you sense a depth of sadness and longing that immediately moves through your heart center. Her sadness wells up in YOU and at once you see through her eyes and have a sense of the suffering she feels for both humanity and all of sea life. You see the heart wrenching polluting of her waters, the fish and sea birds that are covered in oil and waste and the indiscriminate damning up of water flows that leave no safe home for her sea family.

You feel her guilt and deep shame, as she is part human, for causing so much pain and suffering to the waters and its life and her deep longing to walk among humanity, show them the effects of their detached natures and restore respect and care for all living things.

Your and her emotions move as one as you feel HER sorrow for both fish and human and you want nothing more than to ease her suffering. You gently kneel beside her and reach out, drawing her to you and wrapping your arms about her cold body. You draw up unconditional support from the depths of your emotional wellspring and enfold her with the intent of unconditional love, compassion and care. You feel her energy strengthen with your loving touch and tears of joy and understanding fall from your eyes as you offer up the very essence of your compassionate nature to this unfortunate. It is within this place that deep connection and transformational love are offered.

As you release her from your embrace, your eyes connect once again. In the space of tragedy and sorrow, you now see hope. You feel her joy in knowing that the memories of what you saw will guide you towards seeking out other humans who will help to preserve and respect her home. You know that the connection you have made with this beautiful Being has transformed you and you feel empowered in being able to offer up your support.

As these realizations permeate your being you lookout towards the ocean and see that the tide has moved across what was sandy shore. Water laps about you and you rise and look out onto the vastness of the ocean. The tide is returning to claim its own and as you step back the mermaid extends her arms in thanks and you watch as she is gently carried back out to sea in the embrace of a large and light filled wave. You stand taking in the beauty of the waters as they move in towards shore and then return to the vastness of the ocean. You are mesmerized by the sheer beauty of this sight and gently close your eyes taking in the sound of the surf and the smell of salty air. You envision the hope that the mermaid will offer to her kind and healing power of the story she will tell of positive interaction with a human.

As the sounds and the smell begin to fade you open your eyes and you are once again surrounded by the blue veil of energy that carried you to this inner sky. As you take a few more deep breaths and fill the intent with awareness of your physical being and return to your physical space, the mist clears and the smells, sounds and sights of the room in which you began our journey floods your senses. You feel the floor beneath you and the chair on which you are sitting. Noises of the mundane world come back filling ear and mind with thoughts of going about the rest of your day or evening.

You take a deep breath in, savoring the vestiges of your astral journey and the insight it provided, and strongly exhale out affirming your oneness with the present moment of physical time and space.

End Thoughts

It is my hope that you have found the information contained in this book useful and that you will use these Pathworkings as Gateways to Understanding the mysteries of Astrological work.

May the Stars shine brightly within all your workings.

Robin

About the Author

Robin Fennelly is a third degree initiate within The Assembly of the Sacred Wheel Tradition and is High Priestess of Oak and Willow Coven within the ASW. Her spiritual journey is strongly rooted in both Eastern philosophy and the Western Magickal systems from which she has formed a core foundation that is diverse in knowledge and rich in spiritual practice.

As a teacher of esoteric studies, she has used Astrology, Hermetic Qabala, Numerology, and Tarot as the foundation of her diverse selection of workshops and writings for more than 20 years. Robin has written articles for The Witches' Voice online community, The Esoteric Tymes e-newslettter and her blog, The Magickal Pen.

Robin is the owner of Holistic Embrace services for mind, body and spirit and provides services such as Tarot readings, Astrology reports, Serenity Nights and other related offerings. She lives in Eastern Pennsylvania and her life is blessed by a 35-year marriage, five children, 2 pets and the opportunity to work in the field of public education.

Contact Information

Website: robinfennelly.com
Email: oawhighpriestess@yahoo.com

Future Volumes in Magickal and Esoteric Studies

The Inner Chamber
Cornerstones of Magickal Practice

Poetry of the Spheres
A Study of the Qabalistic Spheres from the perspective of Western Mystery studies

Awakening the Paths
An Exploration of the Qabalistic Paths of the Tree of Life from the perspective of Western Mystery studies

A Walk Through the Major Arcana
A Study of the Major Arcana of the Tarot

The Midnight Flame
Solar and Lunar Mysteries and Magick

The Sacred Vessel Mysteries
Esoteric Studies and Western Hermetics

Awakening the Energetic SELF
Energetic practice, Anatomy and Protocol

Vessel of Light
An Exploration of Consciousness and SELF-Awareness